"Just as God took Moses to the top of the mountai views of the Promised Land, this book provides a breath insightful overview of the rich content in the Books of Mose straight forward, fast-paced approach keeps readers engaged o 40-day journey to understand the most foundational principles of our faith. As a pastor, I highly recommend this book to anyone who desires a greater understanding of the Bible, regardless of their experience or level of study. It's practical applications, depth of research and well-written prose makes this book a great resource for personal devotion and Bible study."

—Jerry J. Jeter, DMin, Lead Pastor,
RiverLife Church, Bradenton, Florida

"Rice helped me understand the concepts of the biblical covenant and animal sacrifices in the Old Testament, bringing clarity to these challenging issues by pairing the historical text, *Ancient Near Eastern Text Relating to the Old Testament*, with the readable NIV version of the Old Testament. By providing historical and cultural context, the significance of these scriptures come into sharper focus."

—Dale Denham, CEO

"Rice's expertise in the areas of history and biblical knowledge makes this book a standout among Bible studies. As a teacher, I appreciate Rice's ability to explain challenging biblical concepts in an easy-to-understand manner."

—Kim Pasch, teacher and lifelong learner

"I have studied the first five books of the Bible in the past; however, B. Gilbert Rice was able to unfold the books of Moses in an insightful and concise manner that gave me a deeper understanding and a new perspective of these books.

"*Unlocking the Books of Moses* unfolds the first five books of the Bible in such a way that brings relevancy not only to the New Testament but also to today's culture. If you are interested in deepening your relationship with God, *Unlocking the Books of Moses* is for you."

—Richard L. Smith, small-group Bible leader

"I believe that the greatest challenge of the contemporary church in the West is reconciling all of life with God and embracing a holistic faith experience. In *Unlocking the Books of Moses*, B. Gilbert Rice offers a critical piece to that reconciliation and the restoration of coherence. The Bible is often read by Christians as curious faith material to aid us in certain life circumstances but not as a living and active agency of God on the job, at play, or in preparation for worship. Moreover, understanding the unity of the Bible, as it relates to the covenant between God and humanity as this work reveals it, will accelerate any Christian toward the holistic life they were originally created for in Eden. *Unlocking the Books of Moses* is an invitation to the life you were created to live, where your whole life is reconciled to God."

—Dr. Steve Hall, pastor

"I've attended church my entire life, and I am discovering that looking at the Bible through a historical lens helps me see things in a way I've never seen them before. I appreciate Rice's historical knowledge that illuminates the Scriptures in a new and exciting way.

"As a small business owner with a busy schedule, I like the way the book is organized. The short daily readings can be read in ten to fifteen minutes. I highly recommend this book for busy people who appreciate the historical aspect of the Bible."

—Syndee Daugherty, small-business owner

UNLOCKING THE BOOKS OF MOSES

A 40-DAY JOURNEY THROUGH THE FIRST FIVE BOOKS OF MOSES

B. GILBERT RICE

BROOKSTONE
PUBLISHING GROUP
Birmingham, Alabama

Unlocking the Books of Moses

Brookstone Publishing Group
An imprint of Iron Stream Media
100 Missionary Ridge
Birmingham, AL 35242
IronStreamMedia.com

Iron Stream Media serves its authors as they express their views, which may not express the views of the publisher. While all the stories in this book are true, some of the details and names have been changed or deleted to protect the storyteller's identity. All stories are used by permission.

Library of Congress Control Number: 2022910011

Cover design by Hannah Linder Designs

ISBN: 978-1-949856-67-5 (paperback)
ISBN: 978-1-949856-68-2 (ebook)

1 2 3 4 5—26 25 24 23 22

The secret things belong to the LORD our God, but the things revealed belong to us and to our children forever, that we may follow all the words of this law.

—Deuteronomy 29:29

Open my eyes that I may see the wonderful things in your law.

—Psalm 119:18

For the word of God is alive and active. Sharper than any double-edged sword, it penetrates even to dividing soul and spirit, joints and marrow; it judges the thoughts and attitudes of the heart.

—Hebrews 4:12

Contents

Introduction

Have you ever wondered why the New Testament emphasizes the *blood* of Jesus or why Jesus is referred to as the *Lamb* of God? Perhaps you have questioned why innocent lambs were offered up as sacrifices in the Old Testament. *Unlocking the Books of Moses* is a Bible study that strives to provide answers to those questions.

Reconciliation between God and humankind is the unifying theme of the Bible, and the covenant is presented as the instrument of that reconciliation. A greater understanding of the biblical covenant enables all believers to better comprehend the potential relationship that can be established between us and our Creator.

The concept of covenant found in the Bible can be rather foreign to those of us raised and living in Western culture. We might think of covenants as casual agreements. In the ancient Near East, however, covenants were serious agreements with serious consequences if violated.

Because the covenant motif is an integral concept in the Bible, it is important to examine it through the lens of its ancient culture. By analyzing the biblical covenant—and the bloody sacrifices used to seal it—in the light of the customs and rituals of the ancient Near Eastern world, we can gain a more accurate perspective of many biblical themes.

The covenant is one of many New Testament concepts rooted in Old Testament practices, and having a good grasp of the biblical covenant as presented in the books of Moses provides insight into the new covenant which the New Testament declares was inaugurated by the blood of Jesus (Luke 22:20).

The goal of *Unlocking the Books of Moses* is to help you move past isolated stories of Old Testament patriarchs and toward an awareness of the overarching themes of the Bible. Seeing the big picture can provide a foundation for understanding the covenantal history of the people of God. A deeper understanding of the first five books of the Bible has the potential to enhance every person's relationship with God.

The first five books of the Bible have several titles. They are referred to as the *Torah* (which conveys the notion of instruction in Hebrew), as the *Pentateuch* (*penta* means five in Greek), as the Law of Moses, and as the Books of Moses. But no matter the label, the first five books of the Bible are important because they contain foundational concepts that help us gain an accurate understanding of the message of the whole Bible. To fully appreciate the majesty of God is to comprehend the character of God as revealed in the Old Testament.

The Bible reveals the amazing story of how God reaches out to this rebel world and offers a covenant relationship with Himself to all people. By comprehending the narratives recorded in the Bible, we can gain greater clarity about the dynamics of that relationship.

Think About This

The number of people who read the Bible has greatly diminished. While we typically have more free time than many past generations, we generally devote less time to the study of God's Word. Why do you think that is the case? How much time have you spent reading scripture in the past week?

DAY 1

Genesis 1–5

The word *genesis* means origins or beginnings, and the book of Genesis focuses on three major beginnings: (1) the beginning of the world, (2) the beginning of the human race, and (3) the beginning of the children of Israel. Chapters 1–11 contain a selective history of the human race, and chapters 12–50 provide the story of the ancestors of Israel.

While the description of the beginning of the world could fill volumes, the author of Genesis chose to summarize the seven stages of creation in a few words. The first chapter establishes that God created everything.

Genesis goes on to inform us that the first humans dwelled in an idyllic place. "The LORD God had planted a garden in the east, in Eden; and there he put the man he had formed. The LORD God made all kinds of trees grow out of the ground—trees that were pleasing to the eye and good for food" (Genesis 2:8–9).

Genesis tells us "the LORD God" walked in that garden with Adam and his wife, Eve—imagery that depicts the authentic peaceful relationship initially existing between God and these first humans.

The Hebrew word *shalom* is generally translated as peace. The concept of *shalom*, however, involves more than the absence of conflict. *Shalom* at times also indicates authentic harmony and a situation of wholeness and well-being. In the beginning, a primordial state of divine perfection existed, a *shalom*.

The narrative of Genesis informs us that God gave Adam and Eve a single command (2:16–17), and their choice to disobey the single command they had been given (3:6) interrupted the *shalom* with God they had previously experienced. Their act of disobedience constituted rebellion, and that rebellion had enormous consequences—not only were Adam and Eve banished from the garden of Eden (3:23–24), but they also lost the peaceful and harmonious relationship they had previously enjoyed with their Creator.

According to the New Testament, all their descendants have been impacted by that act. The apostle Paul made a profound statement in his letter to the Roman Christians regarding the consequences of Adam's disobedient and rebellious actions:

> Consequently, just as one trespass resulted in condemnation for all people, so also one righteous act resulted in justification and life for all people. For just as through the disobedience of the one man the many were made sinners, so also through the obedience of the one man the many will be made righteous. (Romans 5:18–19)

Genesis 5 lists the offspring of Adam and Eve after that rebellion (often referred to as "the fall of man"), and the sixth chapter details the great wickedness of those descendants: wickedness that greatly troubled the Lord (v. 6). Genesis tells us that the Lord regretted that he made human beings and decided to wipe them off the face of the earth (6:5–7) with the exception of the family of one man—the blameless and righteous Noah.

Verses to Note
Genesis 1:27–31
Genesis 3

Think About This
The Bible indicates that Adam and Eve initially experienced a relationship of harmony and fellowship with God. Genesis 3, however, records the sad story of our first ancestors freely choosing to commit a blatant act of disobedience against the will of their Creator. Why do you think God created humankind with the capacity for free will?

DAY 2

Genesis 6–11

Noah found favor with God due to his righteous and blameless behavior. He was commanded by God to build a vessel that could float and to load it with animals and food. Noah obeyed, and his obedience allowed him and his family to escape the universal flood and the extinction of all other humans existing at that time.

The structure Noah built was approximately 450 feet long (the length of one and a half football fields), 75 feet wide (the width of a six-lane highway), and 45 feet high (taller than a three-story building). Its three decks were divided into compartments, and the boat was coated with pitch, a tar-like substance, inside and out (Genesis 6:14). It would have been a massive rectangular construction, designed to float. We are not told how long it took to construct the ark, but it must have taken a great deal of faith to undertake such a daunting project.

God protected Noah and his family and informed Noah that He was going to establish a covenant relationship with him (Genesis 6:18). It rained steadily for forty days (7:4), but it took quite a bit longer for the waters to dry up. It appears that Noah and his family (and all kinds of animals) were in that ark for approximately a year (7:11; 8:13).

Upon leaving the ark, Moses built an altar upon which he sacrificed a burnt offering (Genesis 8:20). With Noah, a new beginning with humanity was established, and the same instructions that had been given to Adam were given to Noah—he was to be fruitful and increase in number (1:22; 9:1). The covenant concept is mentioned for the first time in the Bible in the account of Noah (6:18).

Covenant is a very important word in the Bible. It is a binding agreement involving obedience and trust. Noah's trust in God was demonstrated by his obedience to God's directive.

Some notable changes took place after Noah exited the ark: humankind was given the responsibility to govern itself, and the lifespans of humans were reduced. While Noah lived to be 950 years old (Genesis 9:29), his descendants' lifespans would be radically reduced (6:3).

Noah's descendants did not live the blameless lives that their ancestor Noah had lived. Although humanity was given a fresh start with Noah, his descendants failed to live up to their divine purpose as God's agents on the earth. And while they are not described as wicked, they are portrayed as arrogant and self-centered (Genesis 11:1–9). One example of their ungodly behavior is their intention to make a name for themselves by constructing a tower that would reach heaven (vv. 3–4).

The Lord responded to their arrogance by confusing their languages and scattering them over the face of the earth (vv. 6–8). Verses 10–32 are devoted to the ancestors of Shem, one of Noah's three sons, and it is noteworthy that Abraham, the father of the nation of Israel, descended from the line of Shem.

Verses to Note

Genesis 6:1–14
Genesis 9:5–17
2 Peter 2:5

Think About This

Noah, a man who lived during a very violent and corrupt period, is described in the Bible as righteous and blameless (Genesis 6:9–10). What do you think are the characteristics that make it possible for some people to rise above a violent and corrupt culture?

DAY 3

Genesis 12–20

The story of Abraham (who was first called Abram) is the story of another new beginning. Abram was chosen by God for the divine purpose of creating a unique beginning, and he was given a mandate by God to leave his home in Ur and begin a journey without knowing where it would lead (Genesis 12:1). The biblical record of Abram's story begins with his obedience to that directive (vv. 4–9).

Ur, Abram's homeland, was a major commercial center in ancient Mesopotamia, and its literature reveals that it had a pantheon of deities. The people of ancient Ur considered Nanna, the moon god, their patron deity. Separating himself from that confusing religious system may have enabled Abram to hear from God with greater clarity. In any case, Abram's obedience to the Lord's directive demonstrated his extreme trust in and submission to the authority of God.

Abram and his descendants were chosen as instruments through whom God could bless all people (Genesis 12:3). God's promises to Abram focused on three things: a relationship, land, and heirs. Abram was told that a great nation would come from him, that he would be blessed, and that all the people on earth would be blessed through him (vv. 2–3, 7). He and his descendants were chosen to be a light to all nations (Isaiah 51:3–4).

However, Abram and his wife, Sarah, were childless and well past child-bearing age. When Abram brought this up, God instructed him to look at the stars and know that someday his descendants would be that numerous (Genesis 15:2–6). However, some doubts surfaced along with Abram's trust in God.

Abram's greatest struggle was the fact that he was old and had no heir. He asked the Lord for a guarantee, saying, "Sovereign LORD, how can I know?" (Genesis 15:8). So the Lord provided Abram with a guarantee in the form of a covenant (v. 18), and the ritual used to seal God's covenant oath involved a well-known ritual of the ancient Near East.

Abram was told to gather several animals, and he was instructed to cut the carcasses in half. Then God caused Abram to fall into a deep sleep, and during that deep sleep, He showed Abram a vision of fire passing between the pieces of those animals (Genesis 15:9–17). That vision put Abram's doubts to rest. While that ritual is unfamiliar to most of us in modern Western cultures, it was a well-known way to guarantee or seal an oath in the ancient Near East.

Writings from Mari, an ancient civilization that existed in the time of Abram, indicate that the ritual for guaranteeing an oath was to kill an animal. There is a letter that tells of an official sent to establish a peace between two parties, Hanu and Idamaras, by slaughtering the foal of an ass.[1]

The Lord appeared to Abram when he was ninety-nine years old and bestowed upon him the covenant name of Abraham, saying:

> I am God Almighty; walk before me faithfully and be blameless. Then I will make my covenant between me and you and will greatly increase your numbers. . . . No longer will you be called Abram; your name will be Abraham, for I have made you a father of many nations. I will make you very fruitful; I will make nations of you, and kings will come from you. I will establish my covenant as an everlasting covenant between me and you and your descendants after you for generations to come, to be your God and the God of your descendants after you. (Genesis 17:1–7)

God then instructed Abraham to undergo the ritual of circumcision as a sign of the covenant between them. The Lord also instructed

[1] James B. Pritchard, ed., *Ancient Near Eastern Texts Relating to the Old Testament* (Princeton, NJ: Princeton University Press, 1969), 482. Hereafter referred to as ANET.

Abraham to have all his descendants undergo the ritual of circumcision (Genesis 17:10–12).

Verses to Note

Galatians 3:7–9, 29
Hebrews 11:8–19

Think About This

Abraham's obedience demonstrated his trust in God, yet Abraham also expressed doubts regarding one of God's promises (Genesis 15:7–8). Is there a promise you long for God to fulfill? Have you ever experienced a season of doubt regarding the promises of God?

DAY 4

Genesis 21–24

At the age of 100, Abraham was finally blessed with the promised heir, Isaac. The name Isaac means "he laughs," and Isaac's mother, Sarah, who was in her nineties when he was born, stated, "God has brought me laughter, and anyone who hears about this will laugh with me" (Genesis 21:6).

God tested Abraham by directing him to sacrifice his long-awaited heir as a burnt offering (Genesis 22:1–2). One can only wonder what went through Sarah's and Abraham's minds when given this directive.

The ever-obedient Abraham met that challenge by going on a three-day journey with his beloved son, Isaac. Upon reaching the region of Moriah, Isaac asked his father, "Where is the lamb for the burnt offering?" (Genesis 22:7). Abraham's answer reflected his trust in God. He said, "God himself will provide the lamb for the burnt offering, my son" (v. 8). And God did just that—providing a ram for the sacrifice and sparing Isaac's life (vv. 9–13).

Isaac remained unmarried for a long time. When he was in his late thirties, his father, Abraham, sent a servant to his relatives in Harran to find a suitable wife for his son. Apparently, Abraham did not wish for the mother of his descendants to be one of the native inhabitants of Canaan.

That servant took with him ten camels loaded with "all kinds of good things," perhaps as presents for the parents of a potential bride (Genesis 24:10). The servant asked the Lord to direct his choice and felt that Rebekah was the one who was to become Isaac's wife. Her family agreed to let her accompany the servant to Canaan to become Isaac's wife (vv. 12–61).

Isaac was forty years old when he and Rebekah married. In arranged marriages, love was not always a factor, but the Bible tells us that Isaac loved Rebekah (Genesis 24:67). It is heartening to read of Isaac (whose mother recently had died) and Rebekah (whose father had previously passed away) were blessed to find one another.

Rebekah was unable to have children for several years; however, after twenty years of childlessness and many prayers, Isaac and Rebekah were blessed with twins, Jacob and Esau (Genesis 25:21–26).

When a famine occurred in Canaan, Isaac made plans to travel to Egypt where food was more abundant. The Lord, however, did not want Isaac to leave the promised land. He appeared to Isaac and said:

> Stay in this land for a while, and I will be with you and will bless you. For to you and your descendants I will give all these lands and will confirm the oath I swore to your father Abraham. I will make your descendants as numerous as the stars in the sky and will give them all these lands, and through your offspring all the nations on earth shall be blessed, because Abraham obeyed me and did everything I required of him, keeping my commands, my decrees, and my instructions. (Genesis 26:3–5)

The Lord also appeared to Isaac another time stating, "I am the God of your father Abraham. Do not be afraid, for I am with you; I will bless you and will increase the number of your descendants for the sake of my servant Abraham" (Genesis 26:24). After God spoke those words to him, Isaac "built an altar there and called on the name of the Lord" (v. 25).

The altars of the ancient world served a different purpose from the altars in churches today. In ancient times, altars functioned as platforms where animals were sacrificed. Isaac's altar-building suggests the offering of a sacrifice that would have been made to seal an oath and confirm his covenant relationship with the God of his father, Abraham.

Verses to Note

Genesis 24:34–53
Genesis 26:24–30
Hebrews 11:17–19

Think About This

God provided a ram for Abraham and Isaac at a critical time. When was a crucial time in your life when you were in need and benefited from the timely provision of God?

DAY 5

Genesis 25–35

When the twins were born to Isaac and Rebekah, Esau was the first twin to come out of the womb. Most people in the ancient Near East practiced primogeniture—upon the death of the father, the firstborn child inherited everything and became head of the household. Although Jacob and Esau were twins, Esau was considered the firstborn.

Jacob, however, desired those firstborn rights, and as an adult he attempted to get that position. Esau arrived home extremely hungry after hunting, and seeing that Jacob had just cooked some stew, he asked for some of it. Jacob agreed to provide Esau the food in exchange for his firstborn rights, and the hungry Esau readily agreed (Genesis 25:29–34).

Later, Jacob tricked his father into giving him the blessing of the firstborn by disguising himself as Esau (Genesis 27:19–30). Hearing of that trickery, Esau became enraged. He let it be known that he planned to kill Jacob once his father, Isaac, had passed away (v. 41). When Rebekah heard of Esau's plan, she sent Jacob to her brother's family in Harran to escape Esau's wrath (27:42–28:5).

During his journey, Jacob stopped to sleep, and he dreamed of a stairway that extended from earth to heaven. On that stairway (or "ladder" as the KJV calls it), Jacob saw angels ascending and descending (Genesis 28:12). What is most significant about that account is that the Lord stood above that stairway and spoke to Jacob, saying:

> I am the Lord, the God of your father Abraham and the God of Isaac. I will give you and your descendants the land on which you are lying. Your descendants will be like the dust

> of the earth, and you will spread out to the west and to the east, to the north and to the south. All peoples on earth will be blessed through you and your offspring. I am with you and will watch over you wherever you go, and I will bring you back to this land. I will not leave you until I have done what I have promised you. (Genesis 28:13–14)

God offered Jacob the covenant relationship, but instead of accepting that offer, Jacob made a vow. He vowed that *if* the Lord would protect and prosper him and he was able to return to his homeland in peace, *then* the Lord would be his God (Genesis 28:20–21).

In the twenty years Jacob lived in Harran, he experienced great prosperity (Genesis 30:43; 31:38), but he eventually wanted to return to the land of his birth. Now a rich and successful man, Jacob left Harran and began his journey to his homeland.

On his journey back to Canaan, Jacob received word that his brother Esau was coming for him with four hundred men. Jacob's first response was fear, followed by strategic planning. After dividing his household into groups to go before him, he prayed and asked the Lord to save him, reminding God that he had been promised his descendants would be like the sands of the sea. Jacob then sent gifts to Esau, hoping to appease his anger (Genesis 32:6–15).

Genesis records that during the night Jacob had a struggle with a mysterious stranger—a divine being (32:24–25). During that struggle, Jacob received the covenant name of *Israel*.

When Jacob finally encountered Esau, he bowed to the ground seven times. Apparently touched by Jacob's show of respect, Esau threw his arms around Jacob's neck, kissed him, and they wept together (Genesis 33:3–4). The condition of the vow Jacob made years earlier had been fulfilled: Jacob had returned to his homeland in peace and safety.

After Jacob was settled in Canaan, God instructed him to go back to Bethel—the place the Lord had initially offered him the covenant relationship, where he had made the conditional vow that had been fulfilled. Jacob was instructed to build an altar there (Genesis 35:1). Jacob stated, "I will build an altar to God, who answered me in the day of my distress and who has been with me wherever I have gone" (35:3).

After Jacob demonstrated his obedience and trust in the Lord by building that altar, God appeared to him and gave him a new name . . . the covenant name of *Israel* (35:10). The Lord also reiterated the promise of land to Jacob and his descendants (vv. 11–12). Throughout the rest of his life, Jacob acted in faith and fulfilled his role as the bearer of the covenant of Abraham and Isaac.

Verses to Note

Genesis 28:10–22

Genesis 35:1–15

Think About This

When we experience great challenges in our lives, we might not sense God's presence during those periods. But afterward, when we look back on such a time, we sometimes see that God was indeed present. Recall a challenging or distressing period in your life when you did not sense God's presence in those moments. How have you recognized in retrospect that God was with you as He was with Jacob during his time of distress?

DAY 6

Genesis 36–50

Genesis 35–45 provide many interesting details (although not all favorable) about Abraham and his descendants. We learn that Jacob had twelve sons and that his favorite son was Joseph. Joseph was given an ornate robe by his father—an item of clothing that made him stand out as the favorite (Genesis 37:3). Because of that favoritism, Joseph's half brothers became extremely jealous and developed a hatred toward him (vv. 4, 11).

When Joseph was seventeen, those half brothers concocted a plan to get rid of him (Genesis 37:2, 18). The brothers even suggested they kill him. Reuben, the eldest brother, however, was able to persuade his siblings to throw Joseph into a pit instead (vv. 20–22). Joseph was stripped of his ornate robe and thrown into a dry cistern.

Later, when a caravan came through on its way to Egypt, the brothers decided to sell Joseph to that group of Midianites for twenty silver pieces (Genesis 37:28). The scheming brothers then slaughtered a goat and dipped Joseph's robe in its blood. When they returned home, they showed the bloodied garment to their father (vv. 31–32), who became inconsolable, ripping his clothes to express his intense grief over the apparent death of his beloved son (vv. 34–35).

Meanwhile, the Midianites sold Joseph to Potiphar, one of the Egyptian pharaoh's officials. Joseph found favor in the eyes of his master and was put in charge of his household. Unfortunately, Joseph was even more favored by the mistress of the house who tried (and failed) to seduce him (Genesis 39:4, 6–12). Potiphar's wife responded to that rejection by telling her husband that Joseph tried to seduce her, a lie that landed Joseph in prison (vv. 13–20).

Joseph was in prison for a long period, but the Lord was with him even in that situation (Genesis 39:21). While in prison, Joseph interpreted the dreams of some of his fellow prisoners, and that eventually brought him to the attention of the pharaoh (Genesis 40).

The narrative of Joseph details how he went from being a beloved son to a slave to a prisoner and then to a high government official (Genesis 40–41). Joseph was seventeen years old when he entered Egypt and was thirty when he entered the service of the pharaoh (v. 46). Thirteen years of slavery and imprisonment preceded his rise to prominence in Egypt.

A severe famine struck the area during the time Joseph was second-in-command in Egypt. Due to the shortage of food, Joseph's father, Jacob, sent ten of his sons to Egypt to buy grain (Genesis 42:1–3), and they ended up in the presence of Joseph, whom they did not recognize because he was older and outfitted in Egyptian regalia. Joseph, however, recognized them (vv. 6–7).

Joseph strategically chose to accuse his brothers of being spies (Genesis 42:9–17). The brothers responded to that accusation by stating they were simply ten sons of one man (v. 13). When they mentioned their father and a younger brother who were still in Canaan, Joseph insisted they verify their statement by bringing their younger brother to appear before him (v. 20).

Benjamin, the youngest brother, was Joseph's only full brother (a son of Rachel, as was Joseph). When Benjamin was finally brought before him, Joseph was overcome with emotion and had to leave the room (Genesis 43:30).

Later, when Joseph finally revealed to his brothers that he was Joseph, the brother they sold to the caravan of Midianite traders, he again was overcome with emotion. Joseph wept so loudly that all the household of Pharaoh heard him, and his brothers were terrified (Genesis 45:1–3). Throwing his arms around his brother Benjamin, Joseph wept unashamedly (v. 14). When the news of the situation reached Pharaoh, he instructed Joseph to have his family move to Egypt (vv. 16–20).

The brothers returned to Canaan and told their father all that had occurred and that Joseph was alive. Jacob did not believe them at first (Genesis 45:25–26), but eventually he became convinced and wanted to go see Joseph (v. 28). Genesis 46 records that a total of seventy people from Jacob's household eventually settled in Egypt.

Verses to Note
Genesis 37:3–4
Genesis 37:23–35

Think About This
Joseph experienced difficult circumstances before the Lord lifted him out of those situations. Do you think Joseph was tempted to feel resentful or bitter toward his brothers after they sold him into slavery or toward Potiphar's wife when she caused him to be imprisoned? Consider a time when you experienced unjust treatment. How were you tempted to feel toward the person or people who wronged you? How does one overcome such a temptation?

DAY 7

Observations on Genesis

There is a dramatic change of pace beginning with chapter 12 of Genesis. While the first eleven chapters briefly summarize the primeval history of the whole world before Abraham arrived on the scene, the second section, chapters 12 through 50, is devoted to one man, Abraham, and his family, often going into great detail about their lives.

By focusing on Abraham and the promises given to him, Genesis provides the people of God with their history and foundation. The main focus of the book of Genesis is the covenant relationships of Abraham, Isaac, and Jacob—the ancestors of Israel.

Circumcision was the sign of the covenant for Abraham and his male descendants. Other nations, such as Egypt, also practiced circumcision (Jeremiah 9:25). The earliest record of male circumcision comes from a bas-relief carving on a tomb from the Egyptian sixth dynasty (2323–2150 BC). There is also an Egyptian stele at the University of Chicago's Oriental Institute dated from the twenty-third century BC that records a man who was circumcised along with 120 other men.[2]

While we cannot definitely say what circumcision symbolized in Egypt, it is plausible that it was a ritual associated with an oath of loyalty to the Pharaoh. Considering that possible cultural context, it may be that Abraham and his descendants were directed to undergo that rite as a symbol of their loyalty to the Lord God.

[2] ANET, 326.

Genesis informs us that altars were built by Noah (8:20), by Abraham (12:8), by Isaac (26:25), and by Jacob (35:7). In the ancient Near East, the ritual of slaughtering an animal on an altar was used to ratify oaths. It is reasonable to conclude that the mention of altars built by those patriarchs indicates the ratification of an oath before the Lord.

During Jacob's struggle (part of which may have involved facing the conditional vow he had made decades earlier), the divine being told him that he would henceforth be called *Israel* (Genesis 32:28).

The King James translation of Genesis 32:28 indicates that the term *Israel* has the connotation of a prince. In ancient and medieval times, princes were people who pledged exclusive loyalty and obedience to a king. It appears that Jacob submitted himself to the authority of God when he accepted the Lord's offer of a covenant relationship and was thus given the covenant name of Israel.

Genesis reports that Jacob sent gifts to Esau and then bowed before him seven times. It is interesting that the Amarna letters (letters from Canaanite rulers to Egyptian pharaohs) often mention "greeting gifts" and symbolically bowing before the pharaoh seven times. Those actions apparently represented submission to the authority of the overlord.

The story of Joseph's transformation from prisoner to second-in-command in Egypt may seem improbable to some, but the history of ancient Egypt lends credibility to the narrative. Increasing numbers of Semites from Canaan had migrated into Egypt's Nile Delta area beginning in the nineteenth century BC. The demise of the Twelfth Dynasty of Egypt after 1800 BC marked a period of decentralization in the Egyptian government, a development that allowed the Semitic immigrants to step into the power vacuum and establish themselves as the rulers of the agriculturally rich Nile Delta.

The native Egyptians contemptuously referred to those Semitic rulers as *Hyksos*, a word that meant "rulers from foreign lands."

Considering Joseph's similar ethnic Semitic background, the Hyksos pharaohs may have been inclined to treat him and his family favorably. And it is also likely that after the Semitic Hyksos rulers had been ousted, the Semitic Israelites would have been regarded with the suspicion depicted in the first chapters of Exodus.

Genesis provides the background for the covenantal history of God's people contained in the Bible. And the narrative of Adam and Eve's disobedience establishes why there exists a need for reconciliation between God and humankind.

Verses to Note
Genesis 46:1–7
Genesis 46:26–27

Think About This

Obedience is an aspect of the covenant relationship, and it is a strong theme in the book of Genesis as well as throughout the Old Testament. However, when we come to the writings of the New Testament, it is the obedience of Jesus that is emphasized.

It is interesting to note that the apostle Paul juxtaposed the disobedience of Adam with the obedience of Jesus, saying, "For just as through the disobedience of the one man the many were made sinners, so also through the obedience of the one man many will be made righteous" (Romans 5:19).

Take a moment to consider the fact that if you are a believer, because of the new covenant (which was inaugurated by the obedient death of Jesus) you are judged as righteous in the sight of God. How does that truth lead you to respond?

DAY 8

Exodus 1–4

The word *exodus* refers to the Israelites' exit from Egypt. The book focuses on two main events: the Israelites' dramatic departure from Egypt and their alliance with God by means of the covenant. Genesis 15:13–14 records that God told Abraham his descendants would be strangers in a foreign land for four centuries. The story in Exodus takes up the narrative of Abraham's descendants after that four-hundred-year period.

Exodus begins by stating that a new ruler was in power in Egypt and that Joseph meant nothing to him (Exodus 1:8) and his descendants no longer held a favored status. It is possible that Jacob's household journeyed to Egypt during the time the Nile Delta was controlled by the Semitic Hyksos rulers. The Hyksos remained in power in the Delta region until the Egyptian Pharaoh Ahmose I (who ruled Egypt from 1549 until 1524 BC) established the New Kingdom and ousted the Hyksos rulers.

If that was the case, the Israelites' change in status after four centuries could have been due to the pharaohs of the new dynasty being suspicious of the Israelites' potential for disloyalty. The Israelites were ethnically Semitic, as were the ousted Hyksos rulers. The goal of Pharaoh's harsh policies seems to have been to weaken and subjugate the Israelites to preclude any revolt against Egyptian authority (Exodus 1:10–14). One of the extreme policies was the order that all male Israelite babies were to be killed (vv. 16, 22).

Israelites cried out to God during that period of harsh oppression. Exodus 2:23–25 says God heard their groaning and "remembered his covenant with Abraham, with Isaac, and with Jacob." God kept his promise to Abraham (3:10–17; 6:2–8), and he chose Moses to lead the deliverance of the children of Israel (chapters 2–3).

Moses was an exceptional and important individual in the history of God's people. He was born during that oppressive period but became uniquely qualified to lead God's people from bondage. Moses's mother hid him as a baby and later placed him in a basket in the Nile River. The floating basket was brought to the attention of the pharaoh's daughter, who adopted the Israelite child. That led to Moses being brought up in the royal palace of Egypt. The book of Acts states, "Moses was educated in all the wisdom of the Egyptians and was powerful in speech and action" (Acts 7:22).

Because children and grandchildren of the pharaohs were educated to be diplomats and administrators, it is reasonable to conclude that Moses was tutored in those skills also. Administrative skills would serve him well when he was faced with the challenge of turning the mixed mob of people who left Egypt with him (Exodus 12:38) into the well-ordered community we read about in Numbers 2. His education in diplomacy would have familiarized him with knowledge of the international treaty format, which he utilized in mediating the covenant ratified at Mount Sinai.

As an adult, after seeing an Egyptian slave master beat a fellow Hebrew, Moses struck that slave master, who died from the blow. To escape punishment for that act, Moses fled to the land of Midian, which was not under the authority of the Egyptian pharaoh at that time (Exodus 2:11–15).

The fugitive Moses settled into the life of a humble shepherd. One day, while watching his father-in-law's flock, Moses saw a bush that appeared to be burning but was never consumed. After getting Moses's attention by that burning bush (Exodus 3:2–3), the Lord informed Moses of the task chosen for him:

> I am the God of your father, the God of Abraham, the God of Isaac and the God of Jacob. . . . I have indeed seen the misery of my people in Egypt. I have heard them crying out because of their slave drivers, and I am concerned about their suffering. So I have come down to rescue them from the hand of the

> Egyptians and to bring them up out of that land and into a good and spacious land, a land flowing with milk and honey. . . . I have seen the way the Egyptians are oppressing them. So now, go. I am sending you to Pharaoh to bring my people the Israelites out of Egypt. (Exodus 3:6–10)

After living in Midian for forty years, Moses was directed by God to go back to Egypt and speak to the pharaoh. Even though a different pharaoh was reigning from the one in charge at the time of his crime, Moses was naturally hesitant to return to Egypt (Exodus 3:11–14; 4:1, 13).

Moses finally agreed to be obedient to the directive of God. He went first to the Israelite elders (Exodus 3:16; 4:29–31) and then to Pharaoh (3:10; 5:1). Moses, accompanied by his brother Aaron, told Pharaoh that the Lord was requiring his worshippers to hold a festival for him in the wilderness (5:1). But Pharaoh said, "Who is the LORD, that I should obey him and let Israel go? I do not know the LORD and I will not let Israel go" (5:2).

Verses to Note

Acts 7:17–36
Exodus 1:1–10
Exodus 3

Think About This

God called Moses to partner with Him in the deliverance of His people from Egypt's bondage. Have you ever felt led by God to do something that seemed too big to accomplish on your own? Were you hesitant? Did you eventually follow that leading, and if so, what part did you play? What part did God take care of?

DAY 9

Exodus 5–14

The pharaoh not only refused Moses's request for the children of Israel to go into the desert to offer sacrifices to their God, but he also made their labors even more burdensome (Exodus 5:1–2, 6–14). The Lord had told Moses that he was not to expect immediate compliance from the pharaoh, saying, "I know that the king of Egypt will not let you go unless a mighty hand compels him. So I will stretch out my hand and strike the Egyptians with all the wonders that I will perform among them. After that, he will let you go" (3:19–20).

The mighty hand of God came in a sequence of ten plagues: water turning to blood, frogs, gnats, flies, livestock pestilence, boils, hail, locusts, darkness, and the death of firstborn Egyptian children (Exodus 7:14–11:10). Those plagues served to demonstrate the power of the Lord to the Egyptians (7:5).

Before the tenth and final plague, God told Moses to instruct the Israelites to perform the Passover ritual. Households were to slaughter a lamb and place the blood of the slain lamb on the doorframe of their homes. The animal was then to be roasted and all the meat was to be eaten that night (12:1–11).

Because the Passover ritual shares many similarities with ancient Near Eastern oath-swearing rituals, we should consider the possibility that the Passover ceremony originally constituted an oath-taking ceremony in which the Israelites pledged their allegiance and loyalty to the Lord to gain His protection. Exodus 12:21–23 tells us the households that had the Passover lamb's blood on their doorframes were promised protection.

The celebration of the Passover was then to be conducted each year (12:14), and it was to be a restatement of their commitment to the covenant relationship.

The night the Passover ritual was first conducted was also the night of the tenth plague, in which firstborn Egyptian children died. Among the dead was the eldest son of the pharaoh (Exodus 12:29–30). The distraught ruler summoned Moses to the palace and demanded that the Israelites leave Egypt immediately (vv. 31–32).

The Israelites had been instructed to be dressed for travel as they ate the Passover meal (Exodus 12:11), and the Israelites fled Egypt the day following the Passover ritual (Numbers 33:3). The Egyptian pharaoh soon regretted the loss of such a large labor force (Exodus 14:5–7) and attempted to bring the Israelites back to Egypt and slavery.

The pharaoh and his army did not arrive at the Israelites' camp immediately. (According to Numbers 33:5–10, the camp at the Red Sea was their sixth location.) When the Israelites were camped at the edge of the Red Sea, they observed the pharaoh's army advancing toward them and were terrified (Exodus 14:9–12).

No one knows the exact location of the miracle at the Red Sea, but the Bible records that a strong east wind drove back the water of the Red Sea, and Israel crossed on dry land. Following the Israelites' crossing, the strong east wind ceased to blow, and the water rushed back, drowning the pursuing army (Exodus 14:21–23).

That dramatic deliverance provided the Israelites with a display of the power and protection of the Lord God, which motivated them to fear the Lord and put their trust in Him and in Moses His servant (Exodus 14:31).

Verses to Note

Exodus 6:6–8

Exodus 12:1–14, 21–28

Psalm 106:1–12

Think About This

At the edge of the Red Sea, the Israelites found themselves in a situation where there seemed to be no way out (Exodus 14:10–12). When was a time you faced a problem to which there seemed to be no good solution?

DAY 10

Exodus 15–18

The dramatic historical event of the deliverance at the Red Sea was memorialized in song, and a section of that song, Exodus 15:1 (NKJV), is still sung today:

> I will sing to the LORD,
> For He has triumphed gloriously!
> The horse and its rider
> He has thrown into the sea!

After that spectacular deliverance, however, the Israelites faced several challenges as they journeyed from Egypt toward the promised land. There were water issues, and the people grumbled and complained (Exodus 15:22–27). They also complained about the monotony of having only manna to eat (16:2–3), and there were attacks from other nomadic people, such as the Amalekites (17:8–16). The Israelites also struggled to live peacefully among themselves.

The book of Exodus depicts Moses as exhausted from settling the many disputes among the people (18:13–15). Apparently, in an endeavor to obtain a peaceful existence for everyone, including himself, Moses restructured the community. Exodus 18:25 informs us that people were placed in groups of thousands, hundreds, fifties, and tens. Those distinct groupings not only provided order and accountability in the community but also assimilated the group of ethnically diverse people that had accompanied the children of Israel out of Egypt into the community (12:38).

On the advice of his father-in-law, Moses set leaders over those new divisions and gave those leaders delegated authority to handle simple disputes that arose, but the difficult cases were brought before Moses (Exodus 18:26).

By means of that radical reorganization, Moses turned a disorganized throng of people into the well-structured community depicted in Numbers 2. While the drastic restructuring of society is summarized in only a few short verses (Exodus 18:25–26; Deuteronomy 1:13–15), it had a major effect on the community.

And to that community Moses presented God's offer of covenant (Exodus 19:3–9). Moses was chosen not only to lead God's deliverance of His people from Egypt's bondage but also to mediate God's covenant relationship with them (chapters 19–24).

The basic tenet of the covenant is "I will be their God and they will be my people." That recurring theme can be found in Exodus 6:7; Leviticus 26:12; Jeremiah 7:23; 11:4; 30:22; 31:33; 32:38; Ezekiel 11:20; 37:27; 2 Corinthians 6:16; Hebrews 8:10; and Revelation 21:3.

Moses would convey to the descendants of Abraham how they would become the *people of God* by using the formal, solemn, and binding treaty format in which the Israelites acknowledged God as their sovereign king and committed themselves to being His loyal and obedient subjects.

Verses to Note

Exodus 15:22–27
Exodus 17:9–13
Exodus 18:25–26

Think About This

When the Israelites started grumbling and complaining about their hardships and Moses's leadership (Exodus 15:24; 16:2), Moses reminded the people that they were "not complaining against [him], but against the LORD" (16:8). Have you ever been in a position of leadership and experienced complaints or criticism? If so, how did you overcome discouragement and avoid leadership burnout?

DAY 11

Exodus 19–24

The same Hebrew word, *berit*, was used for both covenant and treaty. That is significant because as people in a treaty/covenant relationship, the early Israelites understood God was offering them an oath-bound relationship with Him in which they were obligating themselves to render military service as well as exclusive loyalty and total obedience to God's will.

With the discovery and translation of many ancient Near Eastern treaties during the past century, the cultural context of the Sinai covenant has come into sharper focus. When examined in the light of those treaties, the biblical covenant followed the format of the Late Bronze Age (1500–1200 BC) treaty. Archeologists have unearthed many treaties that the great kings made with smaller nations or city-states, and by analyzing the relationships established by those types of secular treaties, we gain greater clarity about the relationship the biblical covenant was intended to establish.

Two basic types of treaties existed in the ancient Near East: the parity treaty (between equal parties) and suzerainty treaty (between parties of unequal rank). In the suzerainty treaty, the more powerful party (the great king) provided protection and granted land, and the less powerful client-state pledged exclusive and total loyalty to the great king as well as military service and tribute.

Because the client-ruler of a vassal state pledged exclusive loyalty to the great king, he and his subjects understood they could only have one sovereign and that to enter into an alliance with another lord would be considered treasonous. The fact that the covenant ratified at Mount Sinai used the format of a suzerainty treaty carries great significance.

Parity treaties contained specific obligations for both parties, whereas suzerainty treaties contained stipulations for only the client-state. The great king did not commit to any specific obligations; he *was simply to be trusted* to protect those who swore loyalty to him. One of the striking elements of the Late Bronze Age suzerainty treaties was the attention given to the past benevolent actions of the great king toward the client-state. Past benefits were listed in the historical prologue section of the treaty and presented as the rational basis for the future trust to be placed on the king. The rational basis for trusting in the Lord in the biblical covenant is presented in the Bible as God's mighty deliverance of His people from Egypt's bondage.

Moses's use of the suzerainty treaty pattern conveyed to the Israelites that they were entering a formal, solemn, and binding relationship with favor (blessings) for faithful obedience to the Lord's will and consequences (curses) for disobedience to it. The use of that format made it clear that the Lord had the legal right to the exclusive loyalty due a monarch. Many ancient people thought nothing about worshipping a pantheon of deities, but people in the ancient world *knew* that a person could only serve one single monarch.

The principal obligations of the Sinai covenant were set out in the Ten Commandments, and the foremost expectation and obligation of the people was their full and exclusive loyalty to their sovereign. "You shall have no other gods before me" embodied that principle (Exodus 20:3).

Verses to Note

Psalm 25:1–10
Proverbs 3:5–6
Hebrews 11

Think About This

One of the primary expectations of the covenant relationship is that we place our trust in God. The historical past deliverance from Egypt's bondage was presented to Israel as a rational basis for future trust. Proverbs 3:5–6 states, "Trust in the LORD with all your heart and lean not on your own understanding; in all your ways submit to him, and he will make your paths straight." When you analyze your relationship with God, how would you rate yourself in the trust department? Do you feel as though you submit to God "in all your ways"?

DAY 12

Exodus 19–24 (continued)

Suzerainty treaties typically contained six classic elements, and we find those same elements in the covenant made at Mount Sinai.

1. *The Preamble*—Exodus 20:2 and Deuteronomy 5:6 record the preamble, identifying the Lord as the suzerain (the great king): "I am the LORD your God."
2. *The Historical Prologue*—In Exodus 20:2 and Deuteronomy 5:6, the Lord also reminds the people that He brought them out of Egypt, out of the land of slavery. As the historical prologue, these words highlight God's past favor toward His people and serve as the basis for their future trust.
3. *The Stipulations*—Exodus 20:3–17 and Deuteronomy 5:7–21 record the specific obligations (the Ten Commandments) the covenant community swore to obey.
4. *The Deposition Clause and Periodic Reading*—Instructions for the covenant document to be deposited in the tabernacle are recorded in Exodus 40:20–21, and the instruction to publicly read it every seven years during the Feast of Tabernacles is recorded in Deuteronomy 31:10–12.

   Copies of treaty documents were typically deposited in the temples of both parties. It is interesting that the Israelites had no temple at the time of the covenant ratification, but detailed instructions were immediately given for the construction of a portable temple to house the covenant document following the ratification of the Sinai covenant (Exodus 25–31; 35–40).

5. *A List of Witnesses to the Oath Sealed the Treaty*—Deuteronomy 4:26 and 30:19–20 record that the Lord called heaven and earth as witnesses to the covenant oath.
6. *Blessings and Cursings also Sealed the Treaty*—Deuteronomy 27:11–28:68 records an extensive list of blessings and curses: blessings that the subjects of the king could expect if they were obedient and cursings that warned them of the consequences for disobedience. While no such list can be found in the book of Exodus, we do find shalom offerings (often designated fellowship or peace offerings) and burnt offerings. The shalom offerings and burnt offerings were the visual symbols of the covenant blessing and covenant cursing components in the biblical covenant (Exodus 24:4–11).

   In the ancient Near Eastern suzerainty treaties, the written curses were often accompanied by visualized curses—a feature that served a useful purpose for the nonliterate populations of ancient times.

   The covenant ratification ceremony that sealed the covenant is described in Exodus 24: burnt offerings and shalom offerings were made, the blood of those sacrificed animals was splashed on the altar, the Book of the Covenant was read, the people swore an oath saying, "Everything the Lord has said we will do" (v. 3), the blood of the sacrificed animals was sprinkled on the people, and then Moses concluded the ceremony by stating, "This is the blood of the covenant that the Lord has made with you in accordance with all these words" (v. 8).

Analyzing the biblical covenant in its cultural context leads to the conclusion that the people of early Israel understood themselves to be entering into a treaty-type relationship with the Lord God.

The basis for the covenant relationship between God and the nation of Israel was the Lord's relationship with and promises to Abraham, Isaac, and Jacob (Exodus 2:24–25). The Israelites swore to be obedient and loyal to God as their king, and their loyalty and obedience was the appropriate response to God's demonstration of love and concern toward them in offering them the covenant relationship.

Some people have attempted to define the Old Testament as "law" and the New Testament as "grace"; however, both concepts are present in both Testaments. An awareness of the cultural background of the Sinai covenant and its *hesed* sheds light on the issue of grace in the old covenant. *Hesed* is a covenant term that conveys the faithful steadfast covenant love inherent in a covenant relationship, and it also includes the concepts of mercy and grace.

Verses to Note

Exodus 20:1–18
Exodus 24:3–17
Psalm 136

Think About This

The covenant mediated by Moses was an outgrowth and extension of God's covenant with Abraham, Isaac, and Jacob many years prior. Moses used the form of an ancient Near Eastern suzerainty treaty to communicate to the Israelites the type of relationship God was offering to them. By using that format, Moses emphasized that obedience to the will of God would demonstrate their loyalty to God, and the Ten Commandments contained the revealed will of God. Try now to list all ten of the commandments.

DAY 13

Exodus 25–40

The detailed instructions for building a portable temple, the tabernacle, in which the covenant/treaty document was to be housed, are contained in Exodus 25–31. Chapter 32 contains the record of the golden calf incident.

While Moses was away from the camp, some of the Israelites—apparently feeling uncertain about the future—reverted to past ways of thinking. Seeking the comfort of a visible representation of a deity, they requested Aaron, the high priest, to create a visible symbol of God for them (Exodus 32:1). Unfortunately, Aaron complied with that request and created a golden calf (vv. 2–4).

In the ancient world, bulls were often used to signify strength. In Egypt, the false deity Apis was represented by a bull. In the Canaanite literature (which was discovered in 1928 at Ras Shamra, the ancient city of Ugarit in Northern Syria), the deity El, the "most high god," is referred to as Bull El.

The golden calf incident may have been precipitated by the ancient tendency toward syncretism—the identification or merging of the deities of one people with the deities of another nation. Perhaps some of the Israelites erroneously identified the Lord God with one of those false deities.

Following the completion of the golden calf, an altar was constructed in front of it, and burnt offerings and fellowship offerings were sacrificed to it (Exodus 32:5–6). The creation and worship of that idol was a blatant violation of the covenant agreement. The second commandment stated: "You shall not make for yourself an image in the form of anything in heaven above or on earth beneath or in the waters below. You shall not bow down to them or worship them; for I, the Lord your God, am a jealous God" (20:4–5). The Israelites' actions enraged both the Lord and Moses (32:7–10).

Although Moses asked for mercy for the sinning people (Exodus 32:11–13), after witnessing their blasphemous actions, he threw down the covenant document, which broke into pieces ((32:19). Moses immediately ordered the idol destroyed and reprimanded Aaron for leading the people into such a great sin (32:20–21).

After a new covenant document was created (Exodus 34:1, 4), Exodus records a profound statement: "The Lord, the Lord, the compassionate and gracious God, slow to anger, abounding in love and faithfulness, maintaining love to thousands, and forgiving wickedness, rebellion and sin" (34:6–7). The Lord is compassionate and abounding in love and faithfulness. He is still willing to forgive His people who truly repent and turn away from previous sinful behavior.

The book of Exodus concludes with the tabernacle being set up (Exodus 40:17–19), the covenant/treaty document being placed in the ark of the covenant (vv. 20–21) and the glory of the Lord filling the tabernacle (v. 34).

Verses to Note

Exodus 32:1–6, 19–21
Exodus 34:6–7
Psalm 106:19–23

Think About This

The event recorded in Exodus 32 constituted a great sin. The recently delivered people of early Israel reverted to past patterns of behavior, which led them into sin. What are ways you have witnessed new believers struggle with leaving old patterns of behavior behind? How have you experienced that type of struggle?

DAY 14

Observations on Exodus

The exodus from Egypt is traditionally dated as taking place around 1446 BC. That date is based on a passage in 1 Kings, which states the building of the temple in Jerusalem began in the fourth year of the reign of Solomon—480 years after the Israelites left Egypt (1 Kings 6:1). The fourth year of Solomon's reign was 966 BC; therefore, 480 years before that event would date the exodus around 1446 BC.

Have you ever wondered how a male Israelite child such as Moses could be brought into the royal household after a pharaoh had issued an order that all male Israelite babies were to be killed? If the woman identified as "Pharaoh's daughter" was Hatshepsut, that would explain how such a unique situation could have occurred.

Hatshepsut, the eldest daughter of the Pharaoh Thutmose I, was married to her half-brother Thutmose II, and when he died, she was appointed regent over Thutmose III (her husband's son by a concubine), a reign that began when Thutmose III was only two years old. She gained enormous power when reigning as co-regent for her minor stepson (from 1479 until 1458 BC). As a woman who never gave birth to a son, Hatshepsut may have considered a baby boy floating in the Nile River a divine gift. Even after Thutmose III reached adulthood, Hatshepsut retained a great deal of influence in Egypt. Her position may have even overshadowed the reign of her stepson, for history records that Thutmose III removed her name from the majority of the monuments and destroyed most of her statues after her death.

That exceptional situation could explain how Moses, an Israelite, could have been brought into the Egyptian palace during a period of extreme oppression for the Israelite people.

Examining the book of Exodus in the light of ancient Near Eastern culture helps us gain clarity about the purpose and function of the covenant/treaty ratified at Sinai. By using the format of a suzerainty treaty, Moses moved early Israel's conception of the Lord out of the religious sphere (with its polytheistic and syncretistic tendencies) and into the political realm (where exclusive loyalty was the norm). That is significant because people in the ancient Near East knew that a person could have only one sovereign and were keenly aware of the exclusive loyalty inherent in that relationship.

After the children of Israel acknowledged the Lord as their king by covenant-treaty, they would have understood that the Lord had the legal standing to be jealous. That's why the word *jealous* is repeatedly used in the Old Testament in connection with the Lord (Exodus 20:5, 34:14; Deuteronomy 4:24; 5:9; 32:16, 21; Joshua 24:19; 1 Kings 14:22).

Verses to Note
Exodus 20:5
Exodus 34:14

Think About This

Moses asked God His name so he could tell it to the descendants of Abraham (Exodus 3:14). We read that God replied "I AM." The Hebrew word that translates as "I AM" is composed of the four Hebrew letters that have as their English equivalents YHWH. Because there are no vowels in Hebrew, we have to guess at the pronunciation of those four consonants.

Years ago, scholars' best guess for the translation of YHWH was Jehovah (the Y and J sounds are the same in Hebrew as are the W and V sounds); however, modern scholars tend to translate YHWH as Yahweh. Because the pronunciation of YHWH is uncertain, most Bible translations have chosen to substitute the phrase "the LORD" whenever YHWH appears in the text. In your reading of the Scriptures, have you noticed the word LORD in capital letters?

DAY 15

Leviticus 1

The book of Leviticus can be challenging to read because it is full of details concerning various rituals that are unfamiliar to us. However, by paying attention to those details, we can gain valuable insights regarding the initial functions of Old Testament sacrifices and the feasts of early Israel.

The book gets its name from the tribe of Levi, one of the twelve sons of Jacob (and Jacob was the grandson of Abraham). Levi's descendants were set apart from the other tribes to minister in the tabernacle, and the book of Leviticus is mainly concerned with the duties of the Levites and priests.

The book opens with details associated with five offerings of early Israel. The two main offerings in early Israel were the burnt offerings and the fellowship/shalom offerings. Those two offerings were the ones used at Mount Sinai to ratify the covenant (Exodus 24:5).

Understanding the function of the sacrifices and the rituals associated with them in early Israel provides a background for reading some of the harsh declarations of Old Testament prophets. Looking at the burnt offerings from the perspective of treaty/covenant curses and fellowship/shalom offerings as representing treaty/covenant blessings shines a light on some of the hard-to-understand pronouncements of the prophets.

Entering a suzerainty covenant/treaty relationship was a solemn experience, and the curses section of ancient treaties spelled out the severe consequences for violating one's oath of obedience to the king. Because the rituals associated with the burnt offerings as detailed in the book of Leviticus mirror some of the visualized curses used to ratify or seal secular treaties, it seems logical to consider burnt offerings as visual representations of treaty/covenant curses and fellowship/shalom offerings as visual representations of treaty/covenant blessings.

The protocols associated with the rituals in burnt offerings and the rituals we find in some Assyrian treaties suggest that in both cases the fate of the animal was a symbolic representation of the fate of anyone who violated (or sinned against) their oath-bound treaty/covenant commitment. The majority of the population of the ancient world could neither read nor write, so vivid visual representations of curses were vital to convey the serious consequences of breaking one's oath of obedience and loyalty to the king.

Although the Assyrian treaties came later in history, the similarities in the curses section of the treaty between the great king Ashurnirari (the ruler of the Assyrian empire) and Mati'ilu (the ruler of his client-nation) are striking. The cursing section of Ashurnirari's treaty contains this entry:

> This spring lamb has been brought from its fold . . . to sanction the treaty between Ashurnirari and Mati'ilu. . . . This head is not the head of a lamb, it is the head of Mati'ilu, it is the head of his sons, his officials, and the people of his land. If Mati'ilu *sins* against this treaty, so may, just as the head of this spring lamb is torn off . . . the head of Mati'ilu be torn off, and his sons [. . .]. This shoulder is not the shoulder of a spring lamb, it is the shoulder of Mati'ilu, it is the shoulder of his sons, his officials, and the people of his land. If Mati'ilu *sins* against this treaty, so may, just as the shoulder of this spring lamb is torn out, and [. . .], the shoulder of Mati'ilu, of his sons, his officials, and the people of his land be torn out. (emphasis added)[3]

As the body of the lamb was torn apart in the Assyrian treaty-sealing ritual, it was clear what fate awaited the ruler, his sons, his officials, and the people of his land should they choose to violate or sin against the treaty. And those visualized curses made it clear to non-

---

[3] ANET, 532–33.

literate subjects that the fate of the spring lamb symbolized what would befall those who violated or sinned against that treaty.

In the rituals associated with the burnt offering, the lambs used for sacrifices were to be a year old (Exodus 29:38). The individual offering an animal for a burnt offering was to place his hand on the head of the lamb (Leviticus 1:4)—an action that indicated a symbolic identification with the animal and its fate. The animal was then slaughtered, cut into pieces, and the pieces burned up in fire (vv. 5–9). That ceremony followed the standard procedures of ancient Near Eastern oath-swearing rituals. Curses especially were important in ancient Near Eastern culture. These self-maledicted oaths served as a sort of guarantee to the agreement.

In Israel's case, the slaughtered animal used for the burnt offering was not only burned up with fire but also cut up into pieces. Against this background, Old Testament prophets not only warned of fire as a consequence of violating the covenant but also of being chopped into pieces (Jeremiah 5:6; 34:18).

Knowing the symbolism behind the burnt offerings can help clarify some of the harsh statements we find in the Old Testament, such as the statement in Psalm 50, which refers to those who made a covenant with the Lord by sacrifice (v. 5) and states, "Consider this, you who forget God, or I will tear you to pieces" (v. 22).

Verses to Note
Leviticus 1
Exodus 24:5–8

Think About This

Some people view the "God of the Old Testament" as being a wrathful deity. The statements in Jeremiah 34:18 and Psalm 50 can offend our sensitivities. How does viewing the burnt offerings from the perspective of ancient Near Eastern culture with its oath-swearing rituals provide you with context for the harsh language used in those passages?

DAY 16

Leviticus 2–10

Fellowship/shalom offerings are referred to as peace offerings in some translations of the Bible. Leviticus 3:1–17 and 7:11–15 inform us that portions of the fellowship/shalom offering were to be eaten by both the individual making the sacrifice and the priests (7:35). This was the only sacrifice where the person who brought the sacrifice ate a portion of its meat.

That type of offering visually conveyed the concepts of peace, fellowship, and the authentic harmonious alliance that was to exist between God and the people who were entering into a covenant relationship with Him. The record of the ratification of the covenant at Mount Sinai depicts fellowship/shalom offerings being made and seventy elders (who represented the people), along with Moses and priests (who represented God), eating a meal together (Exodus 24:9–11).

A common meal such as a fellowship/shalom offering was a typical ancient Near Eastern method of ratifying a peace agreement between two parties. That type of ritual was used to seal an oath between Isaac and Abimelech: "They ate and drank. Early the next morning the men swore an oath to each other" (Genesis 26:28, 30–31). Also, when Jacob and Laban declared a peace between them, they made a covenant (31:44), and accompanying their oath was a sacrifice and a common meal (vv. 53–54).

The burnt offering and the fellowship/shalom offerings were the sacrifices used to ratify the covenant at Mount Sinai (Exodus 24:5) and continued to be offered throughout the history of early Israel as a continual commitment to the covenant relationship. The rituals for several other specialized offerings are also given in Leviticus: the grain offering (Leviticus 2), the sin offering (4:1–5:13), and the guilt offering (5:14–6:7).

Instructions regarding how priests were to conduct themselves as people set apart for service to God are recorded in Leviticus 9. Chapter 10 records the troubling story of Aaron's two sons, who ignored the proper protocol. Instead, they offered unauthorized fire before the Lord. Because of their careless action, "fire came out from the presence of the LORD and consumed them, and they died" (v. 2). The priests were set apart for service to the Lord, and Nadab and Abihu failed to follow His commands. Their careless, disrespectful actions demonstrated a lack of proper respect toward the LORD, the king of the nation.

After the deaths of Nadab and Abihu, the high priest, Aaron, and his two other sons were directed to forego traditional grieving practices (Leviticus 10:6–7). As God's representatives on earth, the priority of Aaron and his sons was to be their agreement with God's judgment rather than a demonstration of grief for those who trespassed against Him.

Verses to Note

Leviticus 7:15, 34
Genesis 31:44, 53–54
Hebrews 10:5–10

Think About This

The two sons of Aaron, Nadab and Abihu, were priests who failed to show respect toward God. The priests and Levites were set apart to teach and communicate the statutes and ways of God to the rest of the covenant community. Therefore, they had a special obligation to keep God's instructions. Do you believe that people called to leadership are held to higher standards than others?

DAY 17

Leviticus 11–25

Yom Kippur is the Hebrew name for the Day of Atonement, and some unique imagery was associated with that day in early Israel. Leviticus 16 is devoted to the rituals associated with the Day of Atonement, the holiest day in Israel's calendar. There were three major elements to the Day of Atonement ceremonies in early Israel.

First, sin offerings and burnt offerings were made by the priest for himself and the people (Leviticus 16:3). The second element was the scapegoat ceremony. Two goats were brought to the tabernacle on that day. The first goat was sacrificed for the sins of the people (v. 15), then the sins of the people were confessed over the second goat, and it was released into the desert (vv. 20–22). On the Day of Atonement, the people were given a clean slate. The third element was the fasting of all the people in the covenant community. They were to avoid all work (v. 29) and "deny" themselves—an expression interpreted to indicate required fasting (v. 31).

It is interesting that the covenant community was required to fast only one day a year but called to feast several times a year. The three major feasts were the Feast of Tabernacles, also called the Feast of Ingathering and Feast of Booths; the Feast of Unleavened Bread, which included the Passover celebration; and the Feast of Harvest, also called the Feast of Firstfruits.

The Feast of Tabernacles was to be celebrated after the Day of Atonement and last seven days. The Israelites were instructed to build tabernacles (booths) and live in them during that week (Leviticus 23:39–43). That activity served as a reminder of early Israel's nomadic period and recalled God's grace and mercy toward them during that time.

The second major feast was the Feast of Unleavened Bread (which followed Passover) and also lasted for seven days (Leviticus 23:5–8). During the feast, the Israelites were to avoid eating any bread made with yeast. Because their departure from Egypt had happened quickly, there had been no time to allow bread to rise. The period without leavened bread served as a reminder of God's mighty deliverance of His people from the bondage of Egypt.

The third main feast was the Feast of Weeks. That festival was called by several names, including the Feast of Harvest, the Feast of the Ingathering, and the Feast of Pentecost. It focused on the blessings the Lord had provided for His people (Leviticus 23:15–22).

The people of God were called to set aside every seventh day as a Sabbath day. It was a day of sacred assembly, and no work was to be done on that day (Leviticus 23:3). Along with the weekly Sabbath day, the covenant community was also to observe a Sabbath year every seventh year. During the Sabbath year, the Israelites were to leave their fields and vineyards unplanted (25:3–7) and cancel debts from fellow Israelites (Deuteronomy 15:1–2). Israel's religious observances set them apart as grateful people who were committed to remembering all the beneficial blessings they had received from the Lord.

Verses to Note
Leviticus 16:34
Romans 3:25
Hebrews 2:17

Think About This
At the start of the new year in Israel, the visual imagery of the scapegoat running into the desert on the Day of Atonement, never to be seen again, vividly communicated to the people of early Israel the concept of a clean slate with God. Consider the usual practice in Western society of making resolutions at the beginning of our new year. What might it be like to begin each new year instead by visualizing a clean slate with God?

DAY 18

Leviticus 10–25 (revisited)

Holiness is a key theme in the book of Leviticus, and the admonition to be holy as the Lord is holy is repeated several times in the book (for example, 11:44–45; 19:2, 24). Holiness is the essence of God's character, and His people are called to emulate that characteristic. Chapters 17, 18, and 19 define ways in which that holiness should be expressed.

God's people were to live among each other with economic parity, and they were instructed to set up practices that would help the most vulnerable members of their community (19:9–10). As part of this goal, the land system that was to be established in Israel was addressed. Leviticus 25:23 records that the Lord stated, "The land must not be sold permanently, because the land is mine and you reside in my land as foreigners and strangers."

To leave people landless in an agriculturally based society is to invite oppression. The land system of early Israel, if adhered to, would have discouraged the rise of wealthy aristocratic landowners and the oppressive vices that often follow. The prohibition against selling inherited property was intended to ensure the preservation of economic parity among the Israelites after they received their land allotment in the promised land.

A Year of Jubilee was to be celebrated every fifty years. During that year, any lands sold were returned to the family that had originally inherited them (Leviticus 25:11–17). The sale of land in early Israel basically amounted to a lease that expired in the Year of Jubilee. Abraham was given the promise of land to his descendants by God (Genesis 15:18–21), and his descendants were therefore responsible to pass on their land to the next generation

The land system of any nation has a profound influence on its social structure. In most nations, those without land were rarely considered the equal of landowners. That was not to be the case in the covenant community. Because all the people of God were His subjects, they were to live with harmony and equity before Him.

The priests and the Levites were not to receive land when the Israelites settled in the promised land. They were told that the Lord would be their inheritance, and as such, they were to be supported by the tribute (the tithe) that was given to the Lord (Numbers 18:20–24).

The tribe of Levi was set apart to be responsible for the unique duties of caring for and transporting all the components and articles of the tabernacle, but Aaron and his descendants were further set apart as the priests of the nation.

Because the priests and Levites were charged with teaching each generation of Israelites "all the decrees the LORD has given them through Moses" (Leviticus 10:11), they needed to be able to read and write. Because they had no land, the priests and the Levites were precluded from having any agricultural pursuits, which afforded time for studying and teaching the words of the Lord. In this way, the priests and Levites became teachers of the precepts of the Lord to all generations.

Verses to Note

Genesis 15:18–21
Leviticus 10:8–10
Leviticus 25:8–19

Think About This

The people of God were tasked with the responsibility to care for what God entrusted to them—land and children. Are you doing enough to care for what God has entrusted to you? What are you doing to impart covenantal principles and values to the next generation?

DAY 19

Leviticus 26–27

Exodus 23 states that no one was to go before the Lord "empty-handed" (v. 15) and that three times a year all the men should "appear before the Sovereign LORD" (v. 17). The festivals not only celebrated the provisions from the Lord, but they were also to be a time when the loyal subjects of the Lord God, their sovereign king, brought Him the tribute of 10 percent (a tithe) due Him as their sovereign.

The concept of a tribute of one-tenth is first mentioned in the narrative of Abraham giving a tenth of his increase to the King of Salem, Melchizedek, who was also a priest of the Most High God (Genesis 14:18–20). The tithe concept is mentioned again in the narrative of Jacob. Genesis records that after Jacob's vision, in which God offered him the covenant relationship, Jacob responded to the offer by stating that if he was able to return safely to his homeland, then he would give God a tenth (28:20–22). The mention of the tribute of a tenth symbolizes the commitment to acknowledge God's sovereign authority after Jacob's conditions were met.

Moses instructed the people of the covenant that a tithe (a tenth) of all their increase of grain, fruit, and animals belonged to the Lord and was holy to the Lord (Leviticus 27:30–32). The New Testament records that Jesus called out the Pharisees who tithed in the extreme (even tithing their garden herbs) but neglected justice and the love of God, stating that they should have practiced the latter without leaving the former undone (Luke 11:42).

Verses to Note
Exodus 23:14–17
Leviticus 23
Leviticus 27:30–34

Think About This

Read what Jesus said about tithing in Luke 11:42. In light of His declaration, how do you feel about the concept of giving a tenth of your income to God?

DAY 20

Leviticus: Verbal Blessings and Cursings

In the ancient Near East, people understood that entering into a treaty or covenant relationship was a serious occasion with benefits for keeping one's oath of obedience and consequences for failing to keep it. The following verbal blessings and curses are recorded in Leviticus:

> *If you follow* my decrees and are careful to obey my commands, I will send you rain in its season, and the ground will yield its crops and the trees their fruit. . . .
> I will grant peace in the land, and you will lie down and no one will make you afraid. . . .
> I will look on you with favor and make you fruitful and increase your numbers, and I will keep my covenant with you.
> . . .
> *But if you will not listen* to me and carry out all these commands, and if you reject my decrees and abhor my laws and fail to carry out all my commands and so violate my covenant, then I will do this to you: I will bring on you sudden terror, wasting diseases and fever that will destroy your sight and sap your strength. You will plant seed in vain, because your enemies will eat it. I will set my face against you so that you will be defeated by your enemies; those who hate you will rule over you, and you will flee even when no one is pursuing you. (Leviticus 26:3–17, emphasis added)

The treaty/covenant relationship was a serious alliance, and the blessings and curses section of the treaty/covenant reinforced the seriousness of the bond.

Verses to Note
Deuteronomy 28:1–19
Deuteronomy 30:1–6
Psalm 1

Think About This

In His Sermon on the Mount discourse, Jesus used the language of blessings, saying that certain people—including those who were merciful, meek, and pure in heart—would be blessed (Matthew 5:3–10). We later read that He declared woes (curses) upon those who were self-centered (Luke 6:24–26). In which of those two categories would you place yourself: merciful or self-centered?

DAY 21

Observations on Leviticus

The ritual slaying of animals by which solemn oaths were ratified was a common practice in the ancient Near East. Animals were slain to depict the blessing aspect of a treaty/covenant relationship. Later, as in the ratification of the Sinai treaty/covenant, the slain animals represented both the blessing and cursing aspects of the agreement. And in the eighth century BC, we find slain animals being used to represent exclusively the cursing aspect of treaties, as in Assyrian treaties of that era.

The burnt offerings and fellowship/shalom offerings that sealed the Sinai treaty/covenant were bloody events. The focus on blood in the Bible, while strange in our Western cultural context, was a well-known symbol in the ancient world that represented oath-bound commitments. The Bible depicts several ways in which ancient people called the fate of the burnt offering upon themselves: the practice of placing the hand on the head of the animal (Leviticus 1:4); the practice of the sprinkling of the blood of the animal on a group (Exodus 24:8); and the practice of walking between the cut-up pieces of the animal (Jeremiah 34:18).

During the old covenant era, the blood of the burnt offerings and fellowship/shalom offerings were symbols of the sealing of the covenant, which reconciled the Israelites to God. In this present age, the new covenant era, Jesus's death—symbolized by His blood (Luke 22:20)—is presented as the means of our reconciliation with God (Romans 3:25; 5:8–11; 2 Corinthians 5:18–19; Ephesians 2:12–13).

The Bible records God's attitude toward Israel's sacrifices during periods that they failed to live by the covenant. In Isaiah 1:11 God said, "The multitude of your sacrifices—what are they to me? . . . I have more than enough of burnt offerings, of rams and the fat of fattened animals; I have no pleasure in the blood of bulls and lambs and goats." And king David stated, "You do not delight in sacrifices . . . you do not take pleasure in burnt offerings" (Psalm 51:16). When reprimanding King Saul, the prophet Samuel asked, "Does the LORD delight in burnt offerings and sacrifices as much as in obeying the LORD? To obey is better than sacrifice, and to heed is better than the fat of rams" (1 Samuel 15:22).

Verses to Note

Jeremiah 7:22

Psalm 51:15–19

Think About This

The rituals of the burnt offerings and the fellowship/shalom offerings were vital in early Israel and became the basis for the original sacrificial system as well as a major tradition in the nation's worship. Sacrifices were used in Old Testament times to ratify and commemorate the covenant, and they were very bloody events.

In the New Testament, the blood of Jesus is connected to the new covenant and our reconciliation with God. Read Luke 22:20; Romans 3:25; and Romans 5:9–10. How is having a context for the function of blood in the ancient Near Eastern treaty and covenant ratification ceremonies helpful in understanding the symbolism and significance of the blood of Jesus as used in those verses?

DAY 22

Numbers 1–10

The book of Numbers takes up the narrative of early Israel where the book of Exodus ended. While our English translations give this fourth book of Moses the title of Numbers, the Hebrew title for this book is “In the Wilderness.”

A month after the tabernacle was erected, preparations began for the twelve tribes to leave Sinai and travel toward their destination. The first ten chapters of Numbers focus on the preparations for their journey, and the latter section of the book records the covenant community’s missteps along that journey. Their missteps and acts of rebellion turned what should have been an eleven-day journey (Deuteronomy 1:2) into a forty-year nomadic period in the wilderness.

The covenant community had lived at Mount Sinai for a year when the Lord gave the signal to move on. During that year, the covenant had been offered and accepted (Exodus 19–24), the tabernacle had been constructed (25–40), the priesthood had been established (28–29), the principles, statutes, and ordinances of the covenant have been given (Exodus 20–23; Leviticus 11–17), and a census taken (Numbers 1).

The numbering of the people by tribes was another important step in organizing the covenant community. The census count did not include the Levites; however, the framework of twelve tribes was still maintained by subdividing the tribe of Joseph into two tribes named after his two sons, Ephraim and Manasseh (Numbers 1:10–53).

The census contains no mention of the diverse ethnic groups that accompanied the Israelites out of Egypt as mentioned in Exodus 12:38, and the absence of those groups indicates the “mixed multitude” (as the KJV describes them) was incorporated into the covenant community. It is possible that the assimilation was accomplished by means of adoption once people of those groups had undergone the ritual of circumcision and had celebrated Passover (vv. 48–49).

Throughout ancient Israel's history, proselytes have been incorporated into the covenant community once they accepted the Lord as their God. Two such examples are Ruth, a former Moabite (and the grandmother of King David), and Rahab, a former Canaanite (and the great-grandmother of King David). Both Ruth and Rahab are named in the genealogy of Jesus (Matthew 1:5).

At its inception, the nation of Israel was a confederation of twelve tribes allied and unified by the covenant. Numbers 7 lists the leaders of those twelve tribes. Along with those twelve leaders, there were also seventy elders (Numbers 11:24). Seventy descendants of Jacob had entered Egypt, including his twelve sons (Exodus 1:1–5), and those numbers provide the governmental framework in early Israel.

Numbers 2 details how those various tribes were camped around the tabernacle. The tabernacle was placed in the center of the community, and the Levites' tents were arranged around the perimeter of the tabernacle. Then the twelve tribes' tents were set up surrounding the Levites—with three tribes bordering each of the four sides. Moses's organizational skills can be seen in the structuring of the covenant community tribes surrounding the tabernacle.

Before beginning their trek from Mount Sinai, the covenant community celebrated its second Passover (Numbers 9:1–5). The same Passover regulations applied to both the foreigners living among them and native-born Israelites (v. 14; Exodus 12:48–49). Once foreign-born proselytes had been incorporated into the covenant community, they were on equal footing with the native-born Israelites.

Exodus 14:19–24 reports that "the angel of God" went before the Israelites on their journey to Mount Sinai in the form of a cloud. And when the tabernacle was set up, that cloud covered it (Exodus 40:34; Numbers 9:15). When the cloud began moving again, Moses was to instruct the people to prepare to move from Mount Sinai (Exodus 40:36–38). The Lord also instructed Moses to make two silver trumpets to signal the people to prepare for a move (Numbers 10:1–2).

After that second Passover, the cloud moved, the trumpets sounded, and the Israelites set out from the Desert of Sinai. And they did so in an orderly fashion, marching according to their tribal divisions (Numbers 10:14–28).

Verses to Note

Number 1:47–54
Numbers 6:22–27
Numbers 9:15–10:13

Think About This

The tabernacle was the center of the early covenant community. We humans sense the need for organization, and we tend to center ourselves around things that are important to us. We generally do it automatically, often without thinking, based on some primal need or force. Think about the places you frequent in your community. What's at the center of your world? Make a list of the top three things your life is centered around. Identify your "tabernacle."

DAY 23

Numbers 11–15

Only three days into the Israelites' journey from Mount Sinai, some people began to complain about the hardships of nomadic existence (Numbers 10:33; 11:1). On that 150-mile journey from Mount Sinai to Kadesh in the Desert of Paran, they complained about the monotony of manna (11:1–6), they challenged the leadership and authority of Moses (12:1–2), and they orchestrated outright rebellion against the Lord's authority regarding His instructions to drive out the Canaanites from the land (13:31–14:4).

Kadesh was only fifty miles from the border of Canaan, and upon reaching Kadesh, Moses sent out twelve men (one from each tribe) to explore Canaan and report back (Numbers 13:1–20). When they returned, most of those men—with the exception of two men, Joshua and Caleb—advised against attacking Canaan because of its fortified cities and very tall and strong-looking inhabitants (13:24–33; 14:5–9).

Swayed by that negative report, many of the Israelites turned against Moses and Aaron and declared they would rather die in the desert than die by the sword in battle (Numbers 14:1–3). The Lord was angered by the people's rebellious attitude and told Moses to let the people know that no one who treated Him with such contempt would ever see the promised land (v. 23). The Bible tells us that generation of Israelites did not see the promised land—all of them (except Joshua and Caleb) died in the desert they claimed to prefer (14:32–35).

The people's refusal to invade Canaan on the Lord's command demonstrated their lack of trust in Him, and that lack of trust, as well as their refusal to provide military service to their king, was a serious violation of the covenant.

Subjects of a great king were expected to provide military service when called upon; to do otherwise was rebellion. Due to the people's choice to rebel against the authority and command of the Lord, their sovereign, they experienced four decades in the wilderness.

The book of Psalms contains a psalm of Moses, in which he asked the Lord to "have compassion on your servants" (90:13). That psalm sounds like a prayer or lament that could have been prayed at many points during Moses's journey with the covenant community. Perhaps it was composed after the community made the regrettable choice to rebel against God's authority recorded in Numbers 14.

Verses to Note

Numbers 11:4–17
Numbers 13:17–14:4
Numbers 14:20–23

Think About This

Moses prayed that God would have compassion upon His servants. When have you felt as though God had compassion upon you? When have you had compassion toward others?

DAY 24

Numbers 16–19

Although the Israelites brought the years of nomadic existence upon themselves by their disobedient and rebellious behavior, many chose to blame Moses for the situation. Korah, a Levite, along with 250 other well-known leaders in the community, spoke against Moses and Aaron and challenged their leadership.

When Moses summoned some of the main leaders to talk with them, they arrogantly refused to appear before him and stated: "We will not come! Isn't it enough that you brought us up out of a land flowing with milk and honey to kill us in the wilderness? And now you also want to lord it over us! Moreover, you haven't brought us into a land flowing with milk and honey or given us an inheritance of fields and vineyards. Do you want to treat these men like slaves? No, we will not come!" (Numbers 16:12–14).

After hearing that statement, Moses directed the people to move away from the tents of those rebellious leaders and said, "This is how you will know that the LORD has sent me to do all these things. . . . If these men die a natural death and suffer the fate of all mankind, then the LORD has not sent me. But if the LORD brings about something totally new . . . and they go down alive into the realm of the dead, then you will know that these men have treated the LORD with contempt" (vv. 28–30). As soon as Moses finished speaking, the ground opened and swallowed all the people who had rebelled against him (v. 31).

In case there was still any doubt about the Lord appointing Moses and Aaron as the leaders of the covenant community, God set up one more scenario to certify their positions. The Lord told Moses to have the leaders of the twelve tribes bring before him twelve staffs of almond wood with their names written on them (Numbers 17:1–2). And Aaron, as the representative of the tribe of Levi, was also to present a staff with his name written on it (v. 3). All those staffs were to be brought to the tabernacle and placed before the ark of the covenant (v. 4), and the Lord said, "The staff belonging to the man I choose will sprout" (v. 5).

The next morning not only had the staff of Aaron sprouted, but it had also blossomed and produced almonds (Numbers 17:8). This miraculous event demonstrated that it was the divine will of God for Aaron to be the leader of the Levitical priests. God instructed Moses to place Aaron's rod in front of the ark of the covenant as a sign for all the rebellious to see (v. 10).

Verses to Note

Numbers 16:1–11
Numbers 17:2–5
Hebrews 9:4

Think About This

God called Moses to lead the deliverance of His people, and yet Moses had to endure repeated complaints about his leadership. Do you think Moses ever grew weary of having his leadership challenged? How should we treat those whom God has placed over us? On the other hand, should people blindly place their trust in a leader? Read Matthew 7:15–20 and reflect on how Jesus said we can recognize false leaders.

DAY 25

Numbers 20–25

The Israelites spent a large portion of their wandering period camped in the vicinity of Kadesh (Deuteronomy 1:46), an area known to have several sizable springs. However, near the end of the forty years of nomadic existence, a shortage of water developed, and the people grumbled again saying, "Why did you bring us up out of Egypt to this terrible place? It has no grain or figs, grapevines, or pomegranates. And there is no water to drink!" (Numbers 20:5). After Moses prayed, God directed him to gather the people together and speak to a particular rock in their presence. Water would pour out of that rock after he spoke to it (v. 8).

Moses and Aaron gathered the community together, but instead of speaking to the rock, Moses struck it and said, "Must we bring you water out of this rock?" (Numbers 20:10–11). Moses was taking credit for the water appearing when the credit belonged solely to God. That declaration later brought regrettable consequences for Moses (Deuteronomy 32:48–52).

As the years in the wilderness neared completion and most of the older rebellious generation had died out, the covenant community came near the border of Canaan again. When they came to the area settled by Amorites, the Israelites asked to pass through their land (Numbers 21:21–22). That request to pass peacefully through that territory was not only denied, but the Amorites also attacked them (v. 23).

The Lord was with the Israelites, however, and gave them victory over the Amorites. They took control of the Amorites' territory (Numbers 21:24–26). That victory led to a notable poem (vv. 27–30), and the report of the conquest reached Canaan and caused the Canaanites to greatly fear the approaching Israelites (Joshua 2:10–11).

When the Moabites heard of Israel's victory over the ferocious Amorites, they, too, were filled with dread (Numbers 22:1–4). As the Israelites approached the land of Moab, their king, Balak, sent for a seer named Balaam to put a curse on the Israelites (vv. 5–7). Although Balaam was tasked to curse Israel, he could not do it. Every time he tried, he ended up pronouncing a blessing on them (chapters 23–24). Balaam finally explained to King Balak that he was unable to curse what God had not cursed (23:8).

The book of Revelation says Balaam "taught Balak to entice the Israelites to sin so that they ate food sacrificed to idols and committed sexual immorality" (2:14). Balaam was interested in receiving his divination fee, and this verse indicates he counseled King Balak on how he could cause the Israelites to bring a curse upon themselves.

The apostle Peter warned the early church about false prophets who introduced destructive heresies and, in their greed, exploited people (2 Peter 2:1). He compared those teachers to the seer Balaam, "who loved the wages of wickedness" (v. 15). Balaam became the prototype for many religious grifters through the ages who exploited vulnerable people.

By participating in the fertility rituals associated with the Moabite worship of Baal, Israel brought a curse upon themselves. Their serious violation of the covenant caused the Lord's anger to burn against them, and He instructed Moses that all who "yoked themselves to the Baal of Peor" were to be killed (Numbers 25:5).

Verses to Note

Numbers 22:2–5
Numbers 23:7–12, 18–26
Numbers 24:3–14
2 Peter 2:15

Think About This

When God was with the Israelites, they were victorious. When God is with us, we, too, can be victorious. The last book of the Bible has a great deal to say about those who overcome and are victorious. Read the following verses: Revelation 2:7, 11, 17, 26 and 3:5, 12, 21.

DAY 26

Numbers 26–34

While the Israelites were camped on the plains of Moab, Moses took another census of the twelve tribes and listed the separate clans in each tribe (Numbers 26:1–51). All the grown men of the first census were dead, except for Moses, Aaron, Joshua, and Caleb (vv. 64–65). This new census counted all the males of the new generation—males who had been younger than twenty at the first census and had been born during the nomadic period.

After the census was completed, Moses turned his attention to how the promised land would be allotted among the tribes. Moses stated that the larger tribes would receive a larger inheritance, and a smaller lot would go to the smaller tribes: "each is to receive its inheritance according to the number of those listed" (Numbers 26:54).

God had told Moses that neither he nor Aaron was allowed to enter Canaan (Numbers 27:12–13), so He commanded Moses to appoint Joshua to succeed him as the leader of the covenant community. Joshua was to stand before Eleazar the priest and the entire assembly, then Moses was to commission him as their new leader. Moses was also commanded to delegate some of his authority to Joshua so the whole community would recognize Joshua's authority (vv. 18–20).

After anointing Joshua as his successor, Moses reviewed the rituals of offerings, the Passover, the Day of Atonement, and the feast days with the new generation of Israelites who would soon possess the promised land (Numbers 28–29).

Impressed with the fertile land on the east side of the Jordan River, the tribes of Reuben, Gad, and part of the tribe of Manasseh requested permission to settle there (Numbers 32:1–5). Moses expressed his concern that they might forget their covenant obligations to the rest of the tribal federation (vv. 6–15). They assured him they would be available to fight until every Israelite had received his inheritance, so Moses granted their request (vv. 16–19).

Moses then appointed twelve new leaders for the tribes (Numbers 34:18–29). Those new tribal leaders were responsible for assigning the inheritance to the Israelites in Canaan (v. 29). Moses explained to the covenant community how the territory of Canaan was to be divided among them.

With God on their side, the issue was not whether they would conquer Canaan but rather what was to happen once the victory was achieved.

Verses to Note

Numbers 27:12–20
Numbers 32:21–24
Numbers 33:1–39

Think About This

God is faithful to His covenant promises, even in the midst of His people's infidelity. God ordains leaders, and He changes leaders. Moses was a great leader, but eventually, Joshua was chosen to lead the people. Do you feel it is important for there to be a change in leadership over time? Have you ever had a leader that was replaced by a new leader? How do you feel when this happens?

DAY 27

Numbers 32–36

While the Israelites camped near the border of Canaan for the second time, the Lord instructed Moses to tell the people that when they invaded Canaan, they were to drive out all the Canaanites, destroy all their images, and demolish all their high places (Numbers 33:51–52). The high places were sites where the Canaanite fertility rituals took place.

The Canaanites are referred to as God's enemies in Numbers 32:21. The religion of the Canaanites had apparently changed a great deal after Abraham lived among them. During Abraham's time, we read about Melchizedek, a "priest of God Most High" (Genesis 14:18). The Old Testament often uses the title of "Most High" to refer to the Lord God worshipped by the Israelites, but by the period of the exodus, the worship of God Most High had been eclipsed by the worship of Baal.

By the time of Moses and Joshua, the Canaanites had developed a confusing mythology. The tablets unearthed from Ras Shamrah reveal that the religion of the Canaanites had more than thirty deities. Their literature portrays Baal as the son of El and portrays Baal as having successfully challenged El's supremacy. There are also several references to El as "Bull El."[4]

The Lord gave the covenant community many warnings about alliances with the native inhabitants of Canaan. The book of Numbers records that the Lord directed them to drive out the Canaanites from the land, cautioning that failure to do so would bring many problems: "But if you do not drive out the inhabitants of the land, those you allow to remain will become barbs in your eyes and

[4] ANET, 129, 131, 132, 143.

thorns in your sides. They will give you trouble in the land where you will live. And then I will do to you what I plan to do to them" (Numbers 33:55–56).

Verses to Note

Nehemiah 9:7–21

2 Corinthians 6:14–17

Think About This

The early Israelites could have saved themselves from a lot of trouble if they had heeded God's warning not to form alliances with His enemies (the Canaanites). Read 2 Corinthians 6:14–17. Who, or what, might God want you to take a step back from?

DAY 28

Observations on Numbers

When some of the Israelites became bored with eating manna, they forgot the oppressiveness of Egypt's slavery and remembered only the tasty foods they had eaten there, such as fish, cucumbers, melons, onions, and garlic (Numbers 11:4–6). As the people of God, it is important to avoid romanticizing the past and to guard against any tendencies to minimize bondage.

While Korah was the leader of the rebellion against Moses recorded in the book of Numbers, there are many references to the "sons of Korah" in the Psalms. Despite their rebellious ancestor, Korah's descendants became great leaders in choral and orchestral music and many powerful poetic psalms are attributed to them. One of the psalms attributed to sons of Korah begins with these words: "Clap your hands, all you nations; shout to God with cries of joy. For the LORD Most High is awesome, the great King over all the earth" (Psalm 47:1–2).

A powerful prayer, and a good example for us to follow, is recorded in the book of Numbers. The LORD told Moses to tell Aaron and his sons, "This is how you are to bless the Israelites. Say to them: 'The LORD bless you and keep you; the LORD make his face shine on you and be gracious to you; the LORD turn his face toward you and give you peace'" (Numbers 6:23–26).

Verses to Note
Psalm 47

Think About This

The LORD told Moses to tell Aaron and his sons, "This is how you are to bless the Israelites. Say to them: 'The LORD bless you and keep you; the LORD make his face shine on you and be gracious to you; the Lord turn his face toward you and give you peace" (Numbers 6:23–26). When have you felt God's face shine upon you?

DAY 29

Deuteronomy 1–3

The book of Deuteronomy is one of the most quoted books in the New Testament. The name of the book originated from two Greek words: *deuteros*, which means second, and *nomos*, which means law. The book of Deuteronomy contains the second giving of the law.

With great passion, Moses called the new generation of Israelites to total loyalty to the Lord and instructed them to obey all the demands of the covenant. He began his first discourse to that new generation by rehearsing the history of the previous four decades in the wilderness. Moses detailed how he had reorganized the covenant community (Deuteronomy 1:9–18), how he had sent out men from each tribe to assess the land of Canaan (vv. 19–25); and how their ancestors had chosen to disregard God's directive to invade the land of Canaan (v. 26). Moses also explained that because the previous generation had not demonstrated their trust in the Lord, they were not permitted to enter the promised land (vv. 32–35). He then highlighted the victories God had recently given His people over the fierce Amorites.

Moses then revealed that he would not be accompanying the people into the land of Canaan, explaining that though he had pleaded with God to allow Him to go into the promised land (Deuteronomy 3:23–25), "the Lord was angry with me and would not listen to me" (3:26).

The setting for this book is the plains of Moab—just miles away from the promised land. Aware that the covenant community would face many challenges as they transitioned from a nomadic existence (all that generation had ever known) into a more agricultural-based economy when they settled in Canaan, Moses instructed this new generation of Israelites in the ways of the Lord to prepare them for the challenges ahead.

In the historical prologue section of ancient treaties, the suzerain boasted of his previous beneficial acts of kindness toward his subjects. In like manner, Deuteronomy 1–4 functions as an updated historical prologue in which Moses reminded the second generation of God's mercy and kindness toward the community.

The Old Testament contains the covenantal history of the people of God up to the time of the promised Messiah. In examining the covenantal history of God's people, we find that not only the failures of their forefathers are recorded but also God's faithfulness despite those failures.

Verses to Note

Deuteronomy 1:1–39
Deuteronomy 3:23–26

Think About This

Moses rehearsed the past history of the covenant community with the new generation of Israelites and called attention to its ancestors' rebellious choices. Against that background, he called for the new generation to make different choices. When you consider the history of your ancestors or parents, when have you or should have you made different choices than previous generations?

DAY 30

Deuteronomy 4–8

After retelling the history of God's benevolent actions on Israel's behalf, Moses turned his attention to the Lord's instructions. "Now, Israel, hear the decrees and laws I am about to teach you. Follow them so that you may live and may go in and take possession of the land the Lord, the God of your ancestors, is giving you" (Deuteronomy 4:1).

Moses emphasized that the covenant community's primary obligation was to serve the Lord with exclusive loyalty. He warned them against making any idols or images of any shape (Deuteronomy 4:15–18). He also cautioned them to avoid worship of the sun, the moon, or the stars (v. 19), explaining that such behavior would not only provoke God's anger but also have severe consequences (vv. 25–27). He went on to say:

> Acknowledge and take to heart this day that the Lord is God in heaven above and on the earth below. There is no other. Keep his decrees and commands, which I am giving you today, so that it may go well with you and your children after you and that you may live long in the land the Lord your God gives you for all time. (Deuteronomy 4:39–40)

Moses outlined the stipulations of the covenant relationship and emphasized the need to recognize the seriousness of entering a covenant relationship with God. They needed to be aware that they were obligating themselves to be obedient to the revealed will of the Lord God, their king.

The Ten Commandments contain the foremost will of God for His people. And Moses reminded the covenant community that they had sworn to do the following: (1) serve only the Lord and avoid anything to do with false deities, (2) avoid all images and never bow to them, (3) avoid using God's name in vain, (4) observe the Sabbath and keep it holy, (5) honor their parents, (6) never murder, (7) never commit adultery, (8) never steal, (9) never provide false testimonies, and (10) never covet their neighbors' possessions or wives (Deuteronomy 5:7–21).

The tangible expression of the covenant community's love and allegiance to God was to be their obedience to those covenant stipulations. In return, God's people could expect the favor and mercy of God.

Moses admonished the people: "So be careful to do what the LORD your God has commanded you; do not turn aside to the right or to the left. Walk in obedience to all that the LORD your God has commanded you, so that you may live and prosper and prolong your days in the land that you will possess" (Deuteronomy 5:32–33). The instruction to be obedient to the will of the Lord is repeated many times in the book of Deuteronomy (6:25; 8:1; 10:12–13; 11:8–9, 22–25; 24:13).

That generation of Israelites was instructed to destroy the Canaanites and all their idols and to avoid intermarriage with the native inhabitants. There was to be a strict division between the Israelites and the Canaanites that was intended to save Israel from the detestable abominations of the Canaanites and their idolatry (Deuteronomy 7:1–3).

Moses told the people to "love the LORD your God with all your heart and with all your soul and with all your strength" (Deuteronomy 6:5) and warned them of the tendency to forget the Lord in their prosperity:

> When the LORD your God brings you to the land he swore to your fathers, to Abraham, Isaac and Jacob, to give you—a land with large, flourishing cities you did not build, houses filled with all kinds of good things you did not provide, wells

> you did not dig, and vineyards and olive groves you did not plant—then when you eat and are satisfied, be careful that you do not forget the Lord, who brought you out of Egypt, out of the land of slavery. (Deuteronomy 6:10–12)
>
> If you forget the Lord your God and follow other gods and worship and bow down to them, I testify against you today that you will surely be destroyed. Like the nations the Lord destroyed before you, so you will be destroyed for not obeying the Lord your God. (Deuteronomy 8:19–20)

Verses to Note
Deuteronomy 5:6–21
Deuteronomy 6:4–14
Deuteronomy 8:17–20

Think About This
It can be easy to turn to God when we need something only to forget about Him in times of prosperity. Think about a time of prosperity in your life. Did you stay as close to God then as you did during a time of need? How could you overcome that tendency and maintain an awareness of God at all times?

DAY 31

Deuteronomy 9–12

Deuteronomy states that God would drive the Canaanites from the land because of their wicked behavior (9:5), and the Israelites were warned against adopting any of the detestable practices of God's enemies. The Canaanites were referred to as enemies of the Lord (Numbers 32:21), and the book of Deuteronomy repeatedly refers to practices of the Canaanites as detestable (Deuteronomy 7:25; 12:31; 18:9, 12; 27:15; 29:17; 32:16). Deuteronomy 12:29–31 says:

> The LORD your God will cut off before you the nations you are about to invade and dispossess. But when you have driven them out and settled in their land, and after they have been destroyed before you, be careful not to be ensnared by inquiring about their gods, saying, "How do these nations serve their gods? We will do the same." You must not worship the LORD your God in their way, because in worshiping their gods, they do all kinds of detestable things the LORD hates. They even burn their sons and daughters in the fire as sacrifices to their gods.

The unspeakable practice of the Canaanites sacrificing children in the fire is also mentioned in Leviticus 18:21 and Deuteronomy 18:10. The book of 2 Kings later records the Israelite King Josiah destroyed the place where child sacrifices took place "so no one could use it to sacrifice their son or daughter in the fire to Molek" (23:10). Along with the detestable practice of child sacrifice, the Canaanites also practiced sexually immoral fertility rituals at their high places.

Not too long ago, all we knew about Canaanite religion was what the Bible told us. But in 1929, a French archaeologist uncovered text dating from the fourteenth century BC at Ras Shamra (the site of ancient Ugarit). From that translated literature, we have learned that the ancient Canaanites considered El (or Il) to be the supreme deity, ruling over the pantheon (a group of deities officially recognized by a culture) and that he was referred to as the sky god.

Baal was another key figure in their pantheon. Canaanite literature refers to Baal as the Rider of the Clouds.[5] The Canaanites came to view Baal as the lord of thunder and rain and regarded him as controlling of the fertility of the ground. Extensive fertility rituals developed in Canaan that were performed at the high places as a means of encouraging Baal to make it rain so the ground would be fertile and produce a good harvest.

The Israelites were instructed to destroy not only all the Canaanites' altars and images but also the high places and the "Asherah poles" (Exodus 34:13; Deuteronomy 7:5 and 12:3). Asherah was a goddess associated with fertility rituals involved in the worship of Baal. Moses felt the need to direct the covenant community: "Do not set up any wooden Asherah pole beside the altar you build to the LORD your God" (Deuteronomy 16:21).

Verses to Note
Deuteronomy 9:4–6
Deuteronomy 9:9–13

Think About This
The LORD instructed Moses to warn the people to avoid the detestable practices of the culture they were about to encounter. When we are not intentional about following the ways of the Lord, we sometimes fall into a comfortable acceptance of detestable cultural norms. Consider the cultural norms of our present-day society. Are there any practices in our modern society that you feel should be avoided?

[5] ANET, 130.

DAY 32

Deuteronomy 13–26

The book of Deuteronomy places a strong emphasis on the covenant community's duty to protect its most vulnerable members. Because Israel was intended to be a community of equality and parity, specific provisions were made for the less fortunate:

> If anyone is poor among your fellow Israelites in any of the towns of the land the Lord your God is giving you, do not be hardhearted or tightfisted toward them. Rather, be openhanded and freely lend them whatever they need. . . . Give generously to them and do so without a grudging heart; then because of this the Lord your God will bless you in all your work and in everything you put your hand to. There will always be poor people in the land. Therefore I command you to be openhanded toward your fellow Israelites who are poor and needy in your land. (Deuteronomy 15:7–8, 10–11)

The Bible reflects that God cares about the most vulnerable in a community. And Moses noted a special function for the tithes every third year: "When you have finished setting aside a tenth of all your produce in the third year, the year of tithe, you shall give it to the Levite, the foreigner, the fatherless and the widow, so that they may eat in your towns and be satisfied" (Deuteronomy 26:12).

In the ancient Near East, the great kings required the vassal rulers of subject people to annually appear before them to bring tribute. In keeping with that tradition, the people of God were to appear before God during the feast days and bring tribute of one-tenth of their increase.

Verses to Note

Deuteronomy 16:16–17
Deuteronomy 18:15–18
Deuteronomy 26:12–15

Think About This

Deuteronomy 15:8 speaks of being openhanded toward the poor and lending them whatever they need. How does your community of faith help those who are vulnerable or struggling?

DAY 33

Deuteronomy 27–31

Moses instructed the elders of the covenant community to conduct a covenant renewal ceremony after they entered the promised land, and he gave precise instructions on how that ceremony was to be set up (Deuteronomy 27).

The people were told to build an altar and to sacrifice burnt offerings and shalom offerings upon that altar after they entered the promised land (Deuteronomy 27:4–7). Moses left instructions for six tribes—Simeon, Levi, Judah, Issachar, Joseph, and Benjamin—to stand on Mount Gerizim and pronounce covenant blessings on the people. He also instructed the other six tribes—Reuben, Gad, Asher, Zebulun, Dan, and Naphtali—to stand on Mount Ebal and pronounce the covenant curses (vv. 12–13). After emphasizing the blessings of obedience, Moses warned them that curses would overtake them if they did not obey God (28:1, 15).

Deuteronomy 29 records the account of the covenant renewal ceremony that took place at that time on the plains of Moab. After summoning all the Israelites of the new generation, Moses reminded them of the Lord's great deliverance of His people from Egypt's bondage (vv. 2–3); he stressed how the Lord had provided for His people in the wilderness (vv. 5–6); and he called upon the people to remember how God had previously given them victory over the fearsome Amorites (vv. 7–9). After that review of the historical events, Moses stated:

> Carefully follow the terms of this covenant so that you may prosper in everything you do. . . . You are standing here in order to enter into a covenant with the LORD your God, a cov-

> enant the Lord is making with you this day and sealing with an oath, to confirm you this day as his people, that he may be your God as he promised you and swore to your fathers, Abraham, Isaac and Jacob. I am making this covenant, with its oath, not only with you who are standing here with us today in the presence of the Lord our God but with those who are not here today. (Deuteronomy 29:9, 12–15)

Moses declared that he had set before the people life and prosperity as well as death and destruction (Deuteronomy 30:15), and he called for the heavens and earth to be witnesses to these blessings and curses (v. 19).

After making a copy of the covenant document (Deuteronomy 31:9), Moses gave the copy to the priests, and they were instructed to read it to all the people every seven years during the Feast of Tabernacles (v. 10). "Assemble the people—men, women and children, and the foreigners residing in your towns—so they can listen and learn to fear the Lord your God and follow carefully all the words of this law. Their children, who do not know this law, must hear it and learn to fear the Lord your God as long as you live in this land you are crossing the Jordan to possess" (vv. 12–13).

Earlier in the covenant renewal ceremony, Moses announced that God had chosen Joshua to succeed him (Deuteronomy 31:1–8). Joshua had served as Moses's assistant for years (Exodus 24:13; Numbers 11:28). He had also been one of the two scouts who had returned from Canaan with a favorable report (Numbers 14:6–9). Joshua, along with Eleazar the priest, was put in charge of dividing the land among the twelve tribes once they entered Canaan (34:17).

Sadly, Moses and Aaron were not allowed to enter the promised land due to their failure to give God the credit for bringing water from the rock at Meribah Kadesh. The Lord, however, allowed Moses to view the promised land from Mount Nebo before he died (Deuteronomy 32:50–52).

Verses to Note
Deuteronomy 27
Deuteronomy 29
Deuteronomy 31:9–10

Think About This

Deuteronomy 31:10–13 informs us that Moses left instructions that the covenant document was to be read every seven years so the people could learn to respect and fear the Lord God. It was his intent that there be an organized effort to teach the covenant principles to each generation so that each generation could learn to respect and fear the Lord God. Consider that directive. How are we as a society imparting biblical principles and values to the upcoming generations?

DAY 34

Deuteronomy 32–34

Moses was one of the earliest and greatest prophets of God. Old Testament prophets functioned similarly to the royal heralds of ancient great kings. Those royal heralds were charged with announcing the king's messages to the people, and often that included warning them of the consequences should they continue in their rebellion. That was part of Moses's duties also.

The Lord had informed Moses that some of the people would fail to walk in His ways, and when they disobeyed, the covenant curses would happen to them, and calamities would fall on the land (Deuteronomy 29:19–22). If anyone questioned why such things happened to them, the answer was to be "because this people abandoned the covenant of the Lord" (vv. 24–25). Moses was instructed to compose a song about those tragic future events and teach it to the people (31:19), a song that is recorded in chapter 32.

One of the themes that emerges in the Bible is that God is faithful to His oath to Abraham despite the frequent faithless behavior of his descendants. Nevertheless, a remnant of Abraham's descendants would always remain faithful.

In Moses's era, Israel was composed of twelve tribes. But the covenantal history recorded in the Old Testament reports that the nation was basically narrowed down to the remnant of one tribe (Judah) after Assyria conquered the Northern Kingdom of Israel and carried away most of the Northern ten tribes (2 Kings 17:5–6, 18). The Bible contains more than forty references to the faithful remnant.

The book of Deuteronomy closes with the account of Moses climbing Mount Nebo and viewing the whole land God was giving to His faithful people. The Lord said to Moses, "This is the land I promised on oath to Abraham, Isaac and Jacob when I said, 'I will give it to your descendants'" (34:4).

From Mount Nebo, Moses, the mediator of the old covenant, would have beheld the northern mountain peaks of the promised land. And the New Testament reports that many centuries later, on one of those mountain peaks, Moses, along with Elijah, stood and spoke to Jesus, the Mediator of the new covenant (Matthew 17:1–3).

Verses to Note

Psalm 25:10
Zechariah 8:6–7
Romans 9:27

Think About This

When Paul wrote in Romans 11:5 that "at the present time there is a remnant chosen by grace" he was talking about present-day believers. The narratives of the Bible are the stories of God's people, and as believers, we are a part of that covenantal history. How would you define grace? Have you experienced grace? How has it changed your attitude or circumstances?

DAY 35

Observations on Deuteronomy

The basis for Israel's relationship with God flowed out of the Lord's love for Abraham's descendants—the people of the covenant community. And the people's obedience to God's revealed will was an appropriate response to His love and protection.

The axial principle of the Ten Commandments is respect. All ten commandments are based on that principle: respect for the Lord God and respect for others in the covenant community. Consider the amazing society that could be created if everyone in a community showed respect to one another and applied the principles found in the Ten Commandments.

In modern Western culture, we generally perceive the Ten Commandments in the context of individuals, but we would do well to consider their impact if a whole society were to live by them. Imagine if there were no murders, no thefts, no adultery, no false witnessing, and no coveting.

Obeying the Ten Commandments, however, did not (and does not) establish the covenant relationship. Obedience to the will of the Lord was (and is) a demonstration of one's loyalty *after* the relationship has been established.

Most pictures of the Ten Commandments portray two tablets with five commandments on each tablet, but most likely, all ten commandments were on one tablet. In keeping with the practice of making two copies of ancient Near Eastern treaty documents, two copies of that legal document would have been made.

The frequently mentioned "two tablets" in the Old Testament (Exodus 31:18; 32:15; 34:1, 4, 29; Deuteronomy 4:13; 5:22; 9:10–11,

17; 10:3; 1 Kings 8:9; 2 Chronicles 5:10) probably refer to the two copies of the covenant document.

The land was taken away from the Canaanites due to their wickedness (Deuteronomy 9:4). The Israelites could have saved themselves many heartaches had they totally driven out the Canaanites when they initially entered the land. However, they were not completely obedient to that command, and it created many problems for future generations (for example, Judges 2:10–13; Jeremiah 7:18–20).

The false deity that the Canaanites called Asherah would later be known as Ishtar. In Babylon and other ancient Near Eastern cultures, Ishtar was venerated as the "queen of heaven." At the time of the prophet Jeremiah, God called out the families who were making cakes to offer to that queen of heaven and sinning against the Lord by doing so (Jeremiah 7:18–20; 44:19–23).

Jeremiah warned the people that because they broke the covenant by following other gods (Jeremiah 11:10), God would bring a disaster upon them they could not escape (v. 11). That devastating disaster came upon them during Jeremiah's lifetime when Babylon decimated the city of Jerusalem and took its inhabitants into captivity (52:4–14).

Jeremiah, however, was inspired by the Holy Spirit to look beyond that tragic event and prophesy about the new covenant God would initiate in the future: "'The days are coming,' declares the Lord, 'when I will make a new covenant with the people of Israel and with the people of Judah'" (Jeremiah 31:31).

Verses to Note

Judges 2:10–13
Jeremiah 7:18–23
Jeremiah 31:31

Think About This

The book of Deuteronomy stresses the importance of knowing and keeping the law. It should be noted that the Hebrew word conventionally translated as "law" is the word *torah*. While we think of the law in terms of a code of rules, the term *torah* has a broader meaning. It implies instruction, guidance, and direction. How is the *torah* of God's Word instructing, guiding, and directing you?

DAY 36

The Books of Moses and the New Testament

The writings of Moses are repeatedly mentioned in the New Testament. The Gospel writers reported that Jesus referred to Moses and his writings many times (Matthew 8:4; 19:8; 23:2; Mark 1:44; 7:10; 10:5; 12:26; Luke 5:14; 16:29–31; 20:37; 24:27, 44; John 5:46; 6:32; 7:19–23).

The apostle Paul also referred to Moses and his writings (Romans 9:15; 10:19; 1 Corinthians 9:9; 10:2; 2 Corinthians 3:7, 13–16; 2 Timothy 3:8). And the book of Hebrews highlights the teachings of Moses as it discusses the differences between the old covenant and the new covenant (Hebrews 3:2–5, 16–19; 7:14; 8:5–6; 10:28; 11:23–28; 12:21).

Familiarity with the writings of Moses is helpful because they provide a context for many of the symbols and rituals referred to in both the Old and New Testaments. As we examine those symbols and rituals from the perspective of their ancient Near Eastern culture, we gain greater clarity about their intended meanings.

One of the most significant symbols in the New Testament is that of Jesus as the Passover Lamb. Recognizing the Passover lambs of Exodus 12:2–3 as initially being involved with the ratification rituals that guaranteed the oath of loyalty to God illuminates the concept of Jesus as the Passover lamb.

The New Testament is full of references to Jesus as the Lamb of God. John the Baptist referred to Jesus as "the Lamb of God, who takes away the sin of the world" (John 1:29); Peter wrote of "the precious blood of Christ, a lamb without blemish or defect" (1 Peter 1:19); and Paul referred to Jesus as our Passover Lamb that had been sacrificed (1 Corinthians 5:7). The book of Revelation contains twenty-five references to Jesus as the Lamb. His obedient death on the cross is symbolized by the imagery of the Passover lamb—as the sacrifice of the Passover lamb in the Old Testament pointed to the ratification of the old covenant, the sacrificial death of Jesus as the Lamb of God in the New Testament points to the inauguration and ratification of the new covenant.

Another significant symbol in both the Old and New Testaments is blood. Because the rituals used to ratify covenants and treaties in ancient times were extremely bloody events, blood became the symbol of covenant-making. The Hebrew idiom for making a covenant was *karat berit*, which translates as "to cut a covenant."

When the New Testament presents the covenant-sealing blood of Jesus as the symbol of our reconciliation with God (Matthew 26:28; Acts 20:28; Romans 5:9–11; Ephesians 2:13; Colossians 1:20; Hebrews 10:19; 1 John 1:7), it does so against that old covenant background. The rituals used to ratify the Sinai covenant shed light on why the blood of Jesus is mentioned in the New Testament in the context of covenant-making (Luke 22:20).

Grasping the concepts found in the first five books of the Bible provides a foundation for understanding the unifying message in the Bible: the reconciliation between God and humanity. The new covenant, inaugurated by the obedient death of Jesus, is now the instrument of that reconciliation.

Verses to Note
Romans 5:9–11
2 Corinthians 5:17–21
Hebrews 9:12–15

Think About This
The blood of Jesus is a prominent theme in many hymns, but some contemporary churches avoid those kinds of songs. Perhaps that change is due in part to the lack of understanding about the symbolism of the blood in the ancient world. What songs or hymns do you know that mention the blood of Jesus?

DAY 37

The Old Covenant and the New Covenant

The entire Bible centers on two covenants and is likewise divided: the Old Testament (the old covenant) and the New Testament (the new covenant). The names given to the two parts of the Bible rest on the principle that the relationship between God and humans is established by covenant.

The Old Testament anticipated a change in the structure and nature of the new covenant after the old covenant was broken, a fact that is clearly evident in Jeremiah 31. The exact words of Jeremiah's prophecy are quoted by the author of the book of Hebrews as he applied them to New Testament believers (Hebrews 8:8–10).

While there are distinct differences between the old and new covenants, it is worth noting that both contain aspects of grace as well as obedience. In early Israel, the covenant relationship was established by oaths of obedience accompanied by the rituals of sacrifices (burnt offerings and fellowship/shalom offerings). While we recognize the emphasis on the aspect of obedience to the law in the old covenant, it is equally important to recognize the grace of God was also present.

In the New Testament era, along with the grace of God, there is also the aspect of obedience. The new covenant was inaugurated and ratified by the obedient death of Jesus on the cross (Philippians 2:8). Under the new covenant, we enter this covenant relationship through our faith in Jesus. But no longer are we to focus on obedience to a code of written laws. We are to have the will of God in our minds and the covenantal principles written on our hearts.

When asked to identify the most important commandment, Jesus provided the axial principles of the commandments. He said, "'Love the Lord your God with all your heart and with all your soul and with all your mind.' This is the first and greatest commandment. And the second is like it: 'Love your neighbor as yourself.' All the Law and the Prophets hang on these two commandments" (Matthew 22:37–40).

In Jesus's discourse on the mountainside (commonly referred to as the Sermon on the Mount), there is the repeated phrase, *It was said . . . but I tell you . . .* (Matthew 5:21–22, 27–28, 31–34, 38–39, 43–44). In that discourse, Jesus was pointing to the revised and updated new covenant with its new structure and new nature that would be inaugurated upon His death. Later, Jesus also invoked the metaphor of new wine needing to be placed in new containers to convey the coming change in the new covenant's structure and nature (Matthew 9:17; Mark 2:22; Luke 5:38).

Verses to Note

Psalm 136
Matthew 22:37–44
Hebrews 8:8–11

Think About This

Jesus spoke of the principles upon which the commandments were based: loving the Father with all our hearts, souls, and minds; and loving our neighbors as we love ourselves. Would you say you have those covenant principles written on your heart? How does having those principles internalized affect your daily life?

DAY 38

The Messiah

The English word *messiah* comes from the Hebrew word *mashach*. which means "anointed one." The word *Christ* comes from the Greek word *christos*, which also means "anointed one."

The first prophet to predict the coming of the Anointed One was Moses (Deuteronomy 18:18), and we find quite a bit written about the coming Anointed One in the books of Isaiah and Jeremiah. The prophet Isaiah wrote:

> For to us a child is born, to us a son is given, and the government will be on his shoulders. And he will be called Wonderful Counselor, Mighty God, Everlasting Father, Prince of Peace. Of the greatness of his government and peace there will be no end. He will reign on David's throne and over his kingdom, establishing and upholding it with justice and righteousness from that time on and forever. (Isaiah 9:6–7)

And the prophet Jeremiah wrote:

> "The days are coming," declares the LORD, "when I will fulfill the good promise I made to the people of Israel and Judah. In those days and at that time I will make a righteous Branch sprout from David's line; he will do what is just and right in the land. In those days Judah will be saved and Jerusalem will live in safety. This is the name by which it will be called: The LORD Our Righteous Savior." (Jeremiah 33:14–16)

That promise was fulfilled in Jesus. And during Jesus's lifetime many would recognize Him as that promised Son of David (Matthew 12:23; 20:30; 21:9; 22:41–44). However, another group anticipated the messianic son of David to be one who would restore the nation of Israel to the former glory it enjoyed during the reign of King David and expected the Messiah to throw off the rule of the Roman government. Their concept of messianic deliverance was limited to overcoming the power of Rome when in reality the delivering power of Jesus is much broader and is to be found in His overcoming the forces of darkness.

Jesus came as Israel's king to renew the relationship between God and humankind by means of the new covenant that was inaugurated and ratified by His obedient and sacrificial death (Luke 22:20; 1 Corinthians 11:25).

The apostle Paul declared that through the sin of one man, Adam, condemnation entered the world, but through the righteous act of one man, Jesus, we can all be deemed righteous by our faith in Him (Romans 5:12, 18–19). Paul went on to say, "For as in Adam all die, so in Christ all will be made alive" (1 Corinthians 15:22).

Adam had been commanded by God *not* to eat of the tree of the knowledge of good and evil (Genesis 2:17)—a command that appears to be a test to discern whether Adam would be what he was created to be: an obedient son. Sadly, Adam failed that test, and his rebellious action had consequences for the whole human race.

Jesus, however, demonstrated His position as the loyal and obedient Son of God throughout His life. He stated His goal was to be obedient to the will of His Father. Obedience characterized His entire life, including the supreme act of obedience in His death on the cross (Philippians 2:8). Where Adam failed, Jesus succeeded.

It is important to note how much the New Testament stresses the obedience of Jesus and records that Jesus declared, "For I have come down from heaven not to do my will but to do the will of him who sent me" (John 6:38). We see evidence of His obedience to the will of God in His prayer in the garden of Gethsemane, "Father, if you are willing, take this cup from me; yet not my will, but yours be done" (Luke 22:42).

Verses to Note
Acts 3:22–26
Romans 3:22–26
Romans 4:5, 22–25
Romans 5:12–19

Think About This

The apostle Paul repeatedly emphasized that it is not our righteousness but our faith in Jesus that causes us to be declared righteous. Paul wrote of justification (the act of being declared righteous) as God's righteousness being imputed to us by our faith in Jesus (Romans 3:21–5:21). Do you ever doubt your identity as a righteous person?

DAY 39

The People of God

While Jesus, the Messiah sent from God, walked upon the earth, His central teaching was the kingdom of God. Jesus began His public ministry by proclaiming, "The kingdom of God has come near. Repent and believe the good news!" (Mark 1:15).

Jesus often spoke about the kingdom of God in parables, and in studying them, you will notice two distinct aspects. There is the *already* aspect—the parables that focus on the kingdom of God in the present age—and there is the *not yet* aspect—the parables that focused on the kingdom of God in the coming age.

It is significant that the New Testament portrays the kingdom of God as having room for people from other nations as well as people from the nation of Israel. Jesus declared, "People will come from the east and west and north and south, and will take their places at the feast in the kingdom of God" (Luke 13:29).

The apostle Paul noted that Isaiah had prophesied that the Messiah would be a light to the gentiles so that God's salvation would reach the ends of the earth (Isaiah 49:6; Acts 13:47; 26:23). And to the gentile Christians of Ephesus, Paul wrote that they were formerly "Gentiles by birth" and "excluded from citizenship in Israel and foreigners to the covenants of the promise" but were now in Christ Jesus (Ephesians 2:11–13).

According to Paul, "This mystery is that through the gospel the Gentiles are heirs together with Israel, members together of one body and sharers together in the promise in Christ Jesus" (Ephesians 3:6). He also wrote, "If you belong to Christ, then you are Abraham's seed, and heirs according to the promise" (Galatians 3:29).

A recurring theme in the Bible is that God will have a people. "I will be their God, and they will be my people" is the basic tenet of the covenant relationship. That concept is repeated throughout the Bible (Exodus 6:7; Leviticus 26:12; Jeremiah 7:23; 11:4; 30:22; 31:33; 32:38; Ezekiel 11:20; 37:27; 2 Corinthians 6:16; Hebrews 8:10; Revelation 21:3).

The people of God are a people who accept the Lord as their king and commit themselves to be obedient to His will. The people of God include those who are reconciled to God by the covenant of peace inaugurated by the obedient death of Jesus. And the people of God can depend on God's promises, mercy, grace, blessings, and protection that are an inherent part of His steadfast covenant love (*hesed*).

The kingdom of God is composed of the people of God—those who acknowledge the rulership of God in their lives and are in a covenant relationship with Him. The theme of God as king is present in both the *covenant* and *kingdom* concepts.

In the Old Testament, the kingship of God was acknowledged by means of the covenant; in the New Testament, the kingdom of God is presented as the realm where the authority of God, our King, is recognized. The Gospels tell us that Jesus instructed His disciples to pray for God's kingdom to come and for His will to be done (Matthew 6:10). There is a direct connection between acknowledging the kingship and authority of God and doing His will.

Verses to Note

Acts 15:12–21
Romans 11:11–32
Galatians 3:7–9
Ephesians 2:11–18

Think About This

Do you belong to Christ? How do you identify as part of the people of God?

DAY 40

Concluding Thoughts

Ancient Israel's covenant relationship with the Lord was understood in terms similar to those of the suzerainty treaties between great kings of empires and their subject vassal nations. After Israel's many failures, God declared that treaty/covenant had been broken (Jeremiah 31:32).

God then inspired the prophets to write about the new covenant He would make in the future and the transforming work God would do in the hearts of His people at the time of that new covenant. The prophet Jeremiah wrote:

> "The days are coming," declares the LORD, "when I will make a new covenant with the people of Israel and with the people of Judah. It will not be like the covenant I made with their ancestors when I took them by the hand to lead them out of Egypt, because they broke my covenant, though I was a husband to them," declares the LORD. "This is the covenant I will make with the people of Israel after that time," declares the LORD. "I will put my law in their minds and write it upon their hearts. I will be their God, and they will be my people." (Jeremiah 31:31–33)

That new covenant was inaugurated by the death of Jesus on the cross.

The Gospel of Luke says after His resurrection, Jesus, the mediator of this new covenant, appeared to two of His disciples on the road to Emmaus: "And beginning with Moses and all the Prophets, he explained to them what was said in all the Scriptures concerning himself" (Luke 24:27). Jesus, the Prince of Peace, was sent to earth to make our reconciliation with God possible and that reconciliation was foretold in the Old Testament.

The apostle Paul tells us:

> For God was pleased to have all his fullness dwell in [the Son], and through him to reconcile to himself all things, whether things on earth or things in heaven, by making *peace* through his blood shed on the cross. Once you were alienated from God and were enemies in your minds because of your evil behavior. But now he has *reconciled* you by Christ's physical body through death to present you holy in his sight, without blemish and free from accusation." (Colossians 1:19–22, emphasis added)

The apostle Paul also declared: "Since we have been justified through faith, we have *peace* with God through our Lord Jesus Christ, through whom we have gained access by faith into this grace in which we now stand" (Romans 5:1–2, emphasis added).

It is interesting to note that at the birth of Jesus, heavenly hosts appeared on earth praising God saying, "Glory to God in the highest heaven, and on earth *peace* to those on whom his favor rests" (Luke 2:14, emphasis added).

Because of His obedient death on the cross, Jesus is able to reconcile us to God and make possible the type of *shalom* peace for those upon whom God's favor rests, those who are willing to put their trust and faith in Him.

The unifying theme of both the Old and New Testaments is *reconciliation*, and the Bible presents the instrument of that reconciliation as covenant. After we are reconciled to God by the new covenant relationship, we are then in a position to have peace with God. And peace is a critical concept in the Bible.

Human beings in our natural state are enemies of God. We inherited a sin nature from our first parents (Adam and Eve) and seem to naturally possess a rebellious nature. Our disposition to please ourselves is often a barrier to a relationship with God. Lacking a relationship with God, we lack peace.

Peace with God comes exclusively through the covenant relationship made possible by the sacrificial death of Jesus on the cross. Jesus told His disciples: "I am the way and the truth and the life. No one comes to the Father except through me" (John 14:6). The apostle Peter restated that claim when the rulers of the Jews, the Sanhedrin, were disturbed by his teachings about Jesus. Peter said of Jesus, "Salvation is found in no one else, for there is no other name under heaven given to mankind by which we must be saved" (Acts 4:12).

It is important to be aware of the fact that there is only one path to reconciliation and peace with God, and that is through Jesus Christ alone.

God's plan for reconciliation is summed up in John 3:16: "For God so loved the world that he gave his one and only Son, that whoever believes in him shall not perish but have eternal life."

Verses to Note

Matthew 7:13–14
John 3:16
John 14:27
John 20:21

Think About This

John 3:16 is one of the most well-known verses in the Bible, and while Christians may be comfortable talking to others about God, many are not always as comfortable talking about Jesus. Why do you think there is a hesitancy to discuss Jesus?

Author's Note

As a young person I was intrigued by the fact that so many churches came to so many varied conclusions using the very same Bible. That awareness motivated me to read the Bible for myself so I could reach my own conclusions about what is required to have a relationship with God.

At the ripe old age of sixteen, I began the daunting task of reading the Bible from cover to cover. As you might expect, I did not comprehend all I read (and I was completely lost when I came to the Old Testament prophets). My greatest takeaway was that Jesus's teachings centered on the kingdom of God—a concept never mentioned in the church of my childhood.

Wanting to better understand what I had read in the Bible, I signed up for courses on the history of ancient Israel when I began my college education. Then I started adding courses on the neighbors of early Israel—the Egyptians, Assyrians, Babylonians, and Sumerians.

The growing appreciation for ancient history resulted in a bachelor's degree in history from California State University, Fresno (CSUF) in 1977. I immediately followed up graduation by working toward a master's degree in history there. Between classes, I sat at a table in CSUF's student center with an open Bible, searching for connections between what I was learning about the culture of the ancient Near East and the culture of ancient Israel as reflected in the Bible.

In CSUF's library I experienced a truly memorable aha moment while reading the *Annals of the Kings of Assyria*. I noticed the language in Assyrian treaties used some of the same terms and phrases I was familiar with from reading the Old Testament—words such as *blessings* and *curses* and *sin*. It seemed strange to see what I considered religious terms in political documents. Surely I was not the first person to notice those similar terms. The Fresno campus of California State University had an amazing array of academic journals dealing with the ancient Near East, and I scoured those journals looking for related articles (well before the availability of internet searches).

Finally, I found an article that mentioned George Mendenhall, who had published *Law and Covenant in Israel and the Ancient Near East*. Mendenhall's book informed me that the structure of ancient Israel's covenant followed the format of Hittite treaties; he also mentioned the book *Ancient Near Eastern Texts Relating to the Old Testament*, edited by James B. Pritchard, in his footnotes.

Feeling as though I had stumbled upon the elusive Holy Grail, I immediately ordered *Ancient Near Eastern Texts Relating to the Old Testament* and devoured all the treaties, underlining sections that paralleled Old Testament concepts and words. After two years of study on the California campus, I ended up finishing my studies in Florida, receiving a master's degree in religious studies from the University of South Florida. I am grateful that the Lord allowed me to learn about Him through the study of His Word as well as examining ancient Near East cultures.

My studies led me to a closer relationship with God, so helping others understand the Bible has been one of my greatest passions. I have spent most of my adult life teaching the Bible in churches and Bible institutes. After retiring a few years ago, I was drawn back to my old college study notes and research papers. That led me to reread *Ancient Near Eastern Texts Relating to the Old Testament* (noting the passages I had underlined years before). Then I began to read the Bible through again and took new notes—notes that became the basis for this book.

It is my sincere hope that this book helps readers gain a better perspective regarding the overarching theme of the Bible. And it is my heartfelt prayer that all who take this 40-day journey into the books of Moses acknowledge God's anointed Messiah, Jesus Christ, as their Lord and Savior and accept the wonderful gift of reconciliation made available through His covenant-sealing blood and His obedient death on the cross.

B. Gilbert Rice